design *in the*
Plant Collector's Garden
from chaos to beauty

design *in the* Plant Collector's Garden

from chaos to beauty

Roger Turner

Timber Press
Portland • Cambridge

All photographs are by Roger Turner, unless otherwise indicated.

Published in 2005 by

Timber Press, Inc.
The Haseltine Building
133 S.W. Second Avenue, Suite 450
Portland, Oregon 97204, USA

Timber Press
2 Station Road
Swavesey
Cambridge CB4 5QJ, UK

Designed and produced by Hilton/Sadler, London

Printed through Colorcraft Ltd., Hong Kong

Library of Congress Cataloging-in-Publication Data

Turner, Roger.
 Design in the plant collector's garden: from chaos to beauty / Roger Turner.
    p. cm.
  ISBN 0-88192-690-6 (hardback)
 1. Landscape plants. 2. Gardens—Design. 3. Landscape gardening. I. Title.

SB407.T87 2005
712'.6—dc22   2004059847

A catalogue record for this book is also available from the British Library.

ACKNOWLEDGEMENTS
Grateful thanks are due to Mrs Audrey Cary, Anna Mumford, Louise Abbott, Peggy Sadler and Jonathan Hilton.

    Also to the following garden owners: Mr K. Ashburner, Mrs Margaret Baber, Mr Adrian Bloom, Mr Bob Brown, Mrs Mary Byrne, Mr Peter Chappell, Mr Kim Davis, Mr & Mrs Brian Dudley, Mr Gary Dunlop, Lady Gibbs, Mrs Diana Grenfell, Mrs Isabel Grindley, Mr Roger Grounds, Mr & Mrs Peter Heaton, Mr & Mrs James Hepworth, Mrs Elaine Horton, Lady Mary Keen, Mr Mike Lang, Mrs Valerie Merritt, Mr Dennis Moorcraft, Mr & Mrs R. Paice, Mr & Mrs M. Pearce, Mr Paul Picton, Mr & Mrs Guy Rasch, Mr David Richards, Mr Chris Searle, Mrs R. Titterington and Mr Don Witton.

    Also to Abbotsbury Gardens, Batsford Arboretum, Beth Chatto Gardens, Bressingham Gardens, Cambridge University Botanic Garden, Coughton Court, Dyffryn Gardens, The Garden House, Lakeland Horticultural Society, Myddleton House Gardens, Ness Botanic Gardens, Sir Harold Hillier Gardens, National Trust gardens: Biddulph Grange, Dunham Massey, Hidcote, Moseley Old Hall, Sissinghurst Castle, Sizergh Castle, Stourhead, Trelissick and Upton House; Pershore College, R. H. S. Garden, Rosemoor, R. H. S. Garden, Wisley, Royal Botanic Gardens, Kew, University of Oxford Botanic Garden, Waterperry Gardens and Westonbirt Arboretum.

PREVIOUS SPREAD The yellow daisies of *Heliopsis* 'Loraine Sunshine', with *Crocosmia* 'Spitfire' and deep blue *Geranium* 'Rozanne' at Bressingham Gardens, near Diss, Norfolk.

Contents

Preface

Plants and gardens form an ideal pair of interests, one might think. Surely these two belong naturally together, and anyone interested in one will necessarily be drawn to the other? But in practice they can be surprisingly hard to reconcile. Interesting plants don't always make a good garden, it seems, and well-laid out gardens don't always contain very exciting plants. Maybe we choose plants with one part of our brains and make gardens with another.

Plants induce a sense of wonder and amazement at the beauty of nature—think of *Hemerocallis*, for example. "Beauty for a day" is the meaning of the generic name. How can nature be so profligate as to produce such wonderful flowers, and allow them to last only one day? Then there is the kudos of owning and successfully growing a rare plant that no one else may have. On the other hand, an attractive garden is also a pleasure to own, with places to sit, paths to stroll along, good plants to admire, and attractive views to be seen from the windows of the house, not to mention the admiration that the garden owner will receive for the good taste and sound judgement that went into its making.

Most gardeners can see the argument that plants in the garden deserve to be arranged with as much artistry as flowers in a vase. At their workplace people sit in meetings, looking intelligent, "proactively" discussing how the next six months of their business should go. Why is it that they come home and allow the project nearest to their heart be the product of random accident? Some people are terrified of the "D" word. In fact, the moment the gardener makes a decision to place two plants together because the effect looks good, a small "design" decision has been made.

In the best gardens, design and plantsmanship complement each other, and exist to mutual advantage. Plant-collecting and garden-making may use different parts of the brain, but there is no reason why they should not occupy the same head. This book aims to show how a range of straightforward and common-sense ideas can improve the appearance of a garden without limiting in any way the scope to grow a wide range of interesting plants—on the contrary, the plants will be seen to greater advantage.

BELOW One of the things that brings people to gardening in the first place is the beauty of flowers, such as that of *Hemerocallis* 'Borgia Queen' seen here. But most people would agree that a garden needs more than individual flowers in order to be successful.

PART

1

On Plants
and Gardens

1
The plant enthusiast's garden

LIKE A CORNER OF THE KINGDOM of heaven, the plant enthusiast's garden is a place where gardeners bring out of their treasury things new and old—the rare, the ordinary, the unknown, and the well-known. A bit of this, a bit of that, plants and more plants: "all things counter, original, strange; Whatever is fickle, freckled (who knows how?)."[1] Over here is the latest acquisition, small but beautiful and still in its pot—the friend who gave it to us had only this one plant to spare. Over there is the tree we brought from our previous garden. See how it's grown! Today we sit in its shade. In this corner is the shrub that we grew from a cutting taken twenty years ago; the one with the curious pink veins on its leaves, not typical of the species. And in that corner is the *Digitalis* we grew from seeds from Russia, flowering for the first time. Did you ever see such flowers? Did you ever smell such scent?

YOU COULD WRITE A POEM ABOUT IT

This kind of garden is the outcome of daily care and attention. Over the years its owners have nourished and cherished it as if it were their own body, demonstrating a to-have-and-to-hold dedication, "till death do us part". There is nothing short-term about this, no passing fancy. For someone who is passionate about plants, making a garden is not like falling in love in an instant, but like living with someone for a lifetime. There's no quick fix, no easy answers, no move-in, move-out, done-it philosophy. One visit is nothing. You've seen it? That would be like catching a glimpse of a face through the window of a passing limousine. You've seen nothing until you've lived with it day in, day out for a year or two.

Making this kind of garden is not like buying a picture, furnishing a room, or even building a house. This is something you can't go down to a store and buy. Nor can the end product be exactly predicted on day one. Indeed there is no end product, for in this garden there is no arrival, only a succession of days spent travelling hopefully. With furniture, you go off and choose it, bring it home, place it against a

wall in the house, and there it will sit until you move it. But buy a plant, and it will grow year on year, and if it is a tree it may get so large that it will dwarf every other plant in the neighbourhood. With less luck, of course, it might keel over and die, in which case you may well feel some emotion—pain, for instance, or a sense of loss. A feeling of guilt, because perhaps you neglected the poor plant. Or a sense of failure, since you know you could have done better. Making a garden such as this is much more like raising a family than furnishing a house—emotion and involvement are the order of the day. Children grow, but they also answer back. And plants answer back as well—love them and they'll love you back. Ignore them and they may well be as dysfunctional and deprived as unloved children.

has withered, something has died (although we hope not). The spring bulbs are showing and it's not even Christmas. Summer is barely over, yet the cyclamen are in flower. The leaves on one of the trees are turning gold, and we know autumn has arrived. That must mean something. You could write a poem about it.

A LONG-TERM AFFAIR

A few years back I received some peony seeds. Peonies are very easy to grow from seed, but there's one thing you need, and that is patience. The seeds are large, glossy, and easy to handle: I planted them in pots in average well-drained compost, covered them with grit and put them in a shady corner, and waited. After twelve months I might have been forgiven if I thought I'd been sold duff seeds—or maybe concluded that mice had eaten them. But wait: did I read somewhere that in the first year, peonies only grow roots, but not shoots? Give them another year, perhaps. So I waited, and yes, a whole year later there were some small green shoots showing. They were much too small for the garden yet, so I potted them up, one to a pot, and waited another year. And so the process of nurturing and tender loving care went on. Which means that now, every year in early summer I have the wonderful, rare flowers of *Paeonia broteroi* in my garden, in rich pink with bright yellow stamens, a plant you won't see too often as you go garden visiting. I also have the yellow peony, *P. mlokosewitschii*, and others whose names, sadly, I have mislaid. Now the only difference between this and raising children is that I haven't lost track of my children's names (yet).

The task of making this kind of garden is never done. The emotions involved may be worthy of opera, but the time-scale is of soap opera. There is no Grand Finale: it just goes on and on, and you may clap whenever you wish. Just as when you wave your children off to college, you find that you haven't finished yet, so the garden lives on. The pine tree I planted twenty years ago as a sprig, eighteen inches (45 cm) high, is now twenty-five feet (8 m) tall. And where else will I see *Pinus taeda*? It's so rare that it's not even listed in the *RHS Plant Finder*. And it's still growing.

On every day of the year the owners of this kind of garden can walk the length and breadth of their plot and find some new pleasure. Something has grown, something has come into flower, something

BELOW *Paeonia broteroi,* grown from seed, in the author's garden. A rarely seen perennial from Spain and Portugal. The true plant enthusiast doesn't begrudge the time and patience needed to bring rare and beautiful plants to maturity.

BELOW One of the pleasures of gardening is to watch plants develop over the course of weeks and months. Here are the newly unfurling fronds of a *Polystichum setiferum* cultivar growing in the author's garden.

Or consider the merits of growing a euphorbia, as an example of the pleasures of this kind of gardening. *Euphorbia characias* would be a good choice. First of all it doesn't die down in the winter, as many perennials do, making it a good plant to have within sight of the windows of the house, where it will help to make the view of the garden green and clothed throughout the entire year. A slightly more interesting feature, should you decide to venture out into the garden in midwinter, is that the tips of the branches are showing some kind of concentration, as if they were thinking about something. Slowly, so slowly that you can't say when, the tips of the stems tilt over, until after a few weeks they are hooked over at the top, something like a shepherd's crook, and have become knobbly. This means that they are holding

tight little buds, which will become part of the large, upright flowerheads. Slowly these heads unfurl and, as the good weather comes, so the plant develops; every day will bring a change. By late spring the bright yellowy-green flowerheads will be fully formed and look splendid for many weeks, until, in high summer, the flowering stems will have to be cut down. For six whole months we have been entertained by this plant, watching as it changes through the seasons.

Beside my front door is a fern. It's no ordinary fern, but a variety of the soft shield fern, *Polystichum setiferum.* It's an improvement on many other ferns for several reasons. First, it's evergreen, which means you have the green fronds all the year round. Second, it builds year on year into a bigger

and bigger plant. Thirdly, it will give you babies—little fernlets that appear on the undersides of the fronds: these can be potted on to make new plants. But the real reason I have it there is because for five or six weeks in the spring it produces a completely new set of fronds at the top of the plant. To me, this is something worth watching as they appear, tightly curled in the centre of the plant. Gradually they uncurl, and on a daily basis I can watch these lovely, oatmealy-silvery fronds unwrap themselves, and all along each frond the side-fronds uncurl as well, so that for several weeks there is a spectacle. Every time I go in or out of the house I see it. It's alive. It's a bit more eventful than a piece of furniture.

ORDER OR CHAOS?
So what does it look like, the plant enthusiast's garden? The plants are wonderful, we know that—each one looked at in close focus. But the garden as a whole, does it present a pleasing picture?

Well, it depends. The best "plantsman's gardens" are magnificent, but the worst, to be honest, are a bit like junk shops (or perhaps I should be more flattering and call them "old curiosity shops"). There used to be an extraordinary "antique" shop in my own town, whose owner always stood on guard at the

OPPOSITE ABOVE An
abundance of foliage and
flowers in the corner of a
plant enthusiast's garden.

OPPOSITE BELOW
Chaos lurks on the fringes of
this plant-lover's garden.

doorway—no one could get any further in than that. Ask the price of anything on display and he got quite difficult. Ask to see a vase in the window and he became really bad-tempered. When he died, they found room after room in his house packed tight with a random mixture of ordinary junk and price-less treasures, each room locked when it became full. The local museum managed to acquire some of the items from his collection, and now the best of these objects are exhibited to advantage. Now, each one has space around it, instead of being randomly crammed together in unintentional and bizarre juxtapositions. Some of these interesting objets d'art have been exhibited with others of their kind—a cabinet full of "Chinese" vases, for example—while others have been placed in tasteful settings, such as an eighteenth-century sitting room, or an Arts and Crafts bedroom.

It is clear that the owner of this antique shop had an eye for a good object. But placing such treasures in an appropriate or flattering setting didn't interest him. Possession was all. So it is with the gardens of some plant enthusiasts—they consist only of plants, as possessed by the owner, plants and more plants, and that's it. Other gardeners, however, show as much skill in displaying their beautiful and interesting plants as they do in selecting and acquiring them. Collecting is fine, but to make a good garden there has to be more. A little skill in arranging and placing the plants in attractive settings is also needed.

The plants-only garden is easy to caricature. We've all been there. Even before we get into the garden we are tripping over pots—half the garden is still unplanted, it seems. The owners greet us with an apology for the jobs half-done, the uncut lawn, and the weeds that can be seen lurking between the pots and in among the plants. The truth is that the owners haven't noticed the weeds until five minutes before their visitors come. They probably don't see the lawn either. They see only the plants.

These owners are worked off their feet, sowing seeds, taking cuttings, potting up, potting on, and planting out. There is less lawn than when we came last time, we notice that another area of grass has been dug up to make space for the things that really matter—the plants. It is fortunate that they sell plants to garden visitors, or the situation would be even more claustrophobic than it is. Walking through the garden, we find it planted with a dazzling array of perennials, shrubs, climbers, and bulbs, many of which we hesitate to name, although we have seen distantly related ones that were much less rare. There are some labels, but others have been moved by blackbirds or the wind: apparently this does not matter, as the owners know all the names—except that of one particular plant, which we would dearly like to put on our own "Wants List". It is on the tip of their tongues, but, how silly, they just can't think of it at the moment.

Paths that were one-man wide last time we came are now only half-a-man wide, which makes progress slow, especially where the adjoining plants are roses or berberis. Luckily our tour is accompanied, which means that small plants lurking under large ones are drawn to our attention. We also learn about plants that once grew in many locations but have since died. The battles against wind, rain, clay soil, deer, slugs, and rabbits are explained to us,

LEFT A jungle-like scene
of good plants but, like the
gardens of many plant
enthusiasts, this garden
seems to be verging on the
edge of impenetrability.

from the house is bound to deserve a photograph. But no—the intrusion of the neighbour's garage and an electricity pole make it impossible. At last, from a position on the far side of the lawn, we find a shot worth taking, looking back towards the house. But apart from this, general views of the garden seem almost impossible to find.

Left on our own for a moment, when the owner runs to answer the telephone, we find we are slightly lost. Left? Right? No—that goes to the compost heap, while straight on seems to lead to more plastic tunnels. Luckily, the owner returns and guides us safely back to our car. But not before we have gathered up a cluster of pots containing rarities destined for our own garden—some purchased, others pressed generously into our hands.

The truth is that in many cases the enthusiast's garden is not a visitor's experience but an owner's experience. Such gardens are not designed to be visited, but to be lived. They are personal and individual extensions of the people who have made them, and visiting them is like stepping into their private lives. But need this extension of the private life be so private? If so, it could well seem to the rest of us to be an opportunity wasted. If only the owners would put on a visitor's spectacles now and again, they might find a whole new dimension to their garden. It is like the difference between two kinds of diary. One is written solely for the writer's benefit, with abbreviations and bits of shorthand almost impossible for a stranger to decipher, and kept under lock and key. The other kind of diary is written with an eye for posterity, and if the diarist imagines that many years later someone else, a descendant or local

along with the problems of poison spray from adjoining farms, occasional visits from intruding cattle, floods, snow, ice, birds that peck flower buds, birds that uproot sempervivums, birds that eat berries, and visitors who steal cuttings. But see how these gardeners have triumphed (more or less) over adversity. Look on my works ye mighty and despair!

THE VIEWFINDER TEST

All this time we have been busy with the camera, taking shots of interesting plants. But before we go, we consider whether there are a few views of the garden as a whole that would be worth taking. We lift the camera. Sadly, there is a plastic tunnel showing on the left in a view that otherwise would have made a good picture. We wander along the paths and find several admirable plant associations and plant groupings, which we duly photograph. We return to the house—surely the view of the garden as seen

historian, will be perusing what is written, it adds a whole new dimension to the writing.

How do we acquire the skill that will enable us to give the garden this added dimension? I once heard of a party of dedicated plantspeople who went to visit a private garden of some size, partly garden and partly landscape in scale. The visitors arrived and hovered on the lawn, waiting for their hostess to appear, discussing at the plants at the edge of the border beside their feet. Suddenly the owner appeared and, eager for them to appreciate the garden as she had made it, began telling them in a commanding voice: "Don't look down, look up!", which they meekly did. She was right, of course. When we look up we see the garden. When we look down, we see only the plants, and in the plant enthusiast's garden there may well be plenty to admire when we look down, but surprisingly little to be enjoyed when we lift our eyes. All plants, no garden.

A few changes are likely, therefore, when plant-focused owners look up, put on quasi-visitor's glasses, and consider their garden. What does it actually look like? It is easy to preach about what should be done, and say firmly that the sheer quantity of plants can undermine the garden's quality; that the rational way out of this chaos is to be ruthless, dig out the second-rate plants, and keep only the best. Unfortunately, I know I have five different kinds of *Bergenia* in my own small town garden, when one would do, and six different pine trees, which is even greater madness, since they create far too much shade. But how can I kill off babies that I have cosseted and cared for over the years?

STRATEGY OR SERENDIPITY?

A plea to be methodical and systematic is more likely to be acceptable to the keen plant-lover than any suggestion that they cut down on numbers. Some people are very methodical when it comes to horticultural practices—sowing seeds, taking cuttings, or giving a plant the conditions it likes—but are highly resistant to method when it comes to general garden-making. They argue in a cheerful fashion that the random placing of plants throws up as many interesting associations as does careful planning. This is true, and similarly you might meet the love of your life on a number 9 bus. Some people have. But you are much likely to meet them in a setting where you are both comfortable, where your interests coincide, and where ages, jobs, families, and backgrounds are compatible. So it is with plants. A little forethought, a little preplanning about which plants to choose and where they should go, will pay off in the end.

2
Collecting plants

NOBODY SEEMS TO PLAN to become a collector of plants, nor does it happen overnight. If it's a disease, it must be one that creeps up unobserved. First of all, it's necessary to possess a garden of your own. Ownership is definitely an important factor: seeing the plants in someone else's garden is not at all the same thing as having them on your own plot of ground. However, if the love of plants is a malady, it is definitely contagious, and to have a few friends or relations who are keen gardeners can often be the breeding ground where it all begins. Visits to good and great gardens, along with easy access to one of those small but dedicated nurseries, will definitely hasten the development of the complaint.

JUST A LITTLE BIT MORE
If we stumble into plant collecting, how we choose our plants may be equally haphazard. We learn on the job, and what we grow at first is usually a chance matter of whom we know and where our travels take us. To begin with, well-meaning friends will give us all the usual lavenders, santolinas, alchemillas, pieces of *Geranium endressii*, and sprigs of purple sage. Sadly we may also acquire plants that run, seed themselves, and become a menace, which were only given away because the previous owner was happy to get rid of them. We will probably have already bought our hybrid tea roses before a more experienced friend explains that species and old-fashioned roses show better taste. Never mind, they're in the ground now. But are they in the right place? A year or so down the line, we begin to realize that the the position where a plant is placed is rather important. Sun, shade, dry soil or damp, front of border, back

of border—getting these right actually affects the health and growth of the plant. So begins an exercise in musical chairs where for a season all plants change places, as we try to get it right.

But before long we are muttering those dangerous words "Must Have"—a well-known symptom of collector's mania. We keep a secret sheet of paper headed "My Wants List"—a wonderland list, where the end can never be reached, and you have to keep acquiring to stay in the same spot. More plants arrive, and then still more. It is like the interviewer who asked: "And how much money, Mr Rockefeller, does one really need to live comfortably?" "Just a little bit *more*," came the reply. *More* is fine for a starving Oliver, but not when a bank account is obscenely fat, or a garden already over-full.

Along with the garden, the bookshelves will also be filling up: every plant addict I know has at least one bookcase loaded with gardening books. A study of the history of book-purchasing carried out by the patient will usually chart the course of the disease quite accurately. It starts with the bland and innocuous manual that tells the novice which end of a spade to hold, or how to tell a weed from a plant. Next come one or two tempting picture books, birthday presents from well-meaning relatives. Danger begins to lurk when the weighty plant encyclopedia is purchased. Next come the hefty volumes dedicated to perennials, the guide to shrubs, and the dictionary of bulbs. Once these sit on a shelf by the bedside you can almost see the danger lights beginning to flash. When the patient actually prefers to sit up in bed reading these books to lying down beside his or her partner, it's clear that the full-blown disease has

BELOW So which rose would you say was the most beautiful rose in the world? Sadly, not many of us would have the space or resources to collect every possible rose in order to answer the question. This candidate is *Rosa* 'Renaissance'.

taken hold. The final stages of the malady evidence themselves in a row of expensive monographs on genera that particularly interest the patient.

Of course the great advantage of books is not only that knowledge increases, but also that bad weather and inclement seasons need be no obstacle to enjoyment. If the garden is too wet or cold, or indeed too dark to work in, the quest for plant knowledge and plant pleasure can still be pursued from the comfort of an armchair.

KNOWLEDGE, USEFUL AND USELESS

Collecting is all about knowledge. Which is the most beautiful rose in the world? Who can tell me—in truth, no-one? In that case I shall set about growing them all, and then I'll know. Well, I would if I had the time, the space, and the financial resources. This urge to find out is what lies at the root of all scientific endeavour. Science not only studies and describes all the things it discovers, it also sorts them into groups (species, genera, and so on) and creates a system or a

pattern in what seems to be the chaos of the natural world. So in a botanic garden we usually find Order Beds, where the plants are grown in botanically related groups, with all the Umbelliferae grown together, for instance. Similarly at the Royal National Rose Society Gardens, at St Albans, Hertfordshire, the roses have been sorted into classes, so that the Gallicas, the Centifolias, Hybrid Perpetuals, Hybrid Musks and so on are all grown together. This is not only a scientific exercise, which would have all these roses grown in a neutral, value-free manner: taste and critical judgement come into it the moment anyone starts comparing one rose with another. This one, we decide, has beautiful flowers, but it also has stiff, awkward branches. This other one is also attractive, but is prone to a disfiguring disease. Opinions may differ, but among those who have studied these matters for a lifetime it is surprising what a consensus there can be.

But there is some ambivalence about the status of knowledge. Is it a good thing, or not? Adam, you may remember, was given the task of naming all the plants and animals. Whether he did so in Latin or in Hebrew was never recorded, but this was considered a good thing to do. Yet in the corner of the garden lurked the awesome Tree of Knowledge of good and evil, the fruit of which was out of bounds. Some knowledge is fine, it seems, but not too much. The classic example of the dangers of excess knowledge is the German legend of Faust, who sold his soul in order to learn the secrets of alchemy. And with knowledge comes power.

Luckily, the kind of collecting indulged in by plant lovers is of the harmless variety, the equivalent of what is generally deemed "useless knowledge". A friend I was at college with collected useless facts, and specialized in the length of various bridges around the world. Even this is not quite as useless as some forms of collecting I have heard of, perhaps the most bizarre of which is the acquiring of traffic cones. This is particularly suspect theologically, since they have to be stolen from the public domain. There are, it seems, tall ones, short ones, orange ones, red ones, white ones—just like plants, really.

There may be a limit to the number of different traffic cones in the world, but it is soon obvious that to collect every garden plant in the world is an impossibility, even if you own Kew Gardens. In order to be selective, we usually go forward on the Taster Principle. In other words, we grow a selection, a taste, of the various different kinds of plants

BELOW *Tulipa vvedenskyi* in the National Collection at Cambridge University Botanic Garden.

BOTTOM Those plants with funny green flowers—surely nobody else will want to collect them?

available. We plant two, or maybe three trees, depending on the space available, and get a taste of the Tree-growing Experience. We acquire a selection of perennials, a few shrubs, a few climbers. We order a range of bulbs for a taste of tulips, a quota of crocuses, a dabble of daffodils, and so on. This kind of garden—and most gardens are like this—slowly builds up into a general plant collection. At its best the garden could be called an "Eclectic Collection", the word eclectic meaning "selecting, or choosing the best out of everything".

FROM THE GENERAL TO THE PARTICULAR

With some people the urge to collect takes a more serious turn. I'd had a garden of my own for about two years when a "quaint little notion came into my head"—one that eventually became moderately life-changing. It occurred to me that it might be interesting to see how many plants of one genus, or varieties of one species, I could bring together. Looking around for what to choose, I thought that no-one else would want to collect those funny looking yellowy-green plants that flower in late spring, and so I might be able to do something original. And in May 1976 we set out for a distant nursery to buy our first euphorbias. So began a saga that culminated some fifteen years later in being asked to write a book about them, which was eventually co-published by Timber Press in 1995.

As is so often the case, I didn't know exactly what I was letting myself in for. From my reference books and catalogues I thought there were about twenty-five different euphorbias, not likely to overwhelm

BELOW Early days of the euphorbia collection in the author's garden.

BOTTOM The National Collection of euphorbias in the Order Beds at the University of Oxford Botanic Garden.

OPPOSITE *Euphorbia griffithii* growing among a wide range of other perennials in a plant enthusiast's garden.

my smallish garden. Gaining access to the old green Royal Horticultural Society Dictionary of Plants, I discovered there were fifty. I was still undaunted. It was only later I discovered there were two thousand. Luckily many of these were succulents, which I had no interest in, and no greenhouse in which to grow them. A host of other *Euphorbia* species had never been brought into cultivation; indeed many are weeds not worthy of being introduced. But even so my book included about a hundred species, some of which featured a long list of varieties.

The impact of these plants on my small garden was considerable. Eventually, and long before the book came along, I decided there was more to life than euphorbias and I dug most of them up, planted them in pots, and gave them away. This was about the time that Britain's National Council for the Conservation of Plants and Gardens (or NCCPG) was formed, a county-by-county organization of serious garden clubs that encourages plant collections. The hope was that a nearby horticultural college would take on my *Euphorbia* collection. I still grow a lot of euphorbias in my own garden—some particularly good ones, some new ones, and some I still haven't managed to weed out.

GHETTOS AND DIASPORAS

A single-genus collection (or varieties of a single species) is quite a different exercise from an eclectic collection, and raises a range of new problems. To impose on a small garden a large number of plants that look roughly similar can be beneficial, but can also be problematic. There may be a lack of variety: the plants in question may be all the same height, for

example. It's especially difficult to handle a large number of very small plants. For instance, it would be hard to imagine a collection of thymes looking very impressive, especially if they were all planted together in rows. Scattered among various troughs or around a rock garden, they would look fine. But in that case it would then not be so easy to compare one with another.

If all the plants have the same habit, or the same flower colour, leaf colour, or leaf shape, this may cause additional difficulties. Euphorbias, for example, are nearly all yellowy-green in the colour of their floral heads. It could be argued that this will have a unifying effect, but it might equally be considered monotonous. Another problem with a single-genus collection may be that, in one part of the garden at least, everything is liable to be in flower at the same time. A passion for hellebores, for example, if it

starts to run away with you, will produce a garden that is the envy of one's gardening friends in early spring but will have nothing but leaves in summer when other people's gardens are a riot of colour. A large number of plants all dying in unison, or at least past their best, may not be a pretty sight. One advantage of euphorbias is that although many flower in May and June, there will also be species in flower in February, March, April, August, and September.

The basic dilemma at the heart of making a single-genus collection is whether the plants are to be grouped or dispersed. If they are grouped, one plant can be compared easily with another for height, flower size, general performance, garden-worthiness and so on. But if they are dispersed, they will show to greater advantage in the garden and the problems of monotony will be avoided, but comparisons will be more difficult to make.

3
Making a general collection

GIVEN THE OPPORTUNITY of a new start on virgin territory, the keen gardener usually insists on bringing along van-fulls of plants from the previous garden, all of them evidently indispensable. Usually some kind of economic reasoning is used—it would be such a pity, we tell ourselves, to have to spend money buying them all over again. I know all about this from experience.

TO PLAN OR NOT TO PLAN

But instead of all that work digging up plants, squeezing them into pots, and replanting them all again, a wholly different enterprise could be undertaken, less demanding physically but possibly more challenging to the brain, the powers of judgement, and the desire to possess. Faced with the overwhelming array of plants that we could grow in, for example, the average temperate garden, we could concentrate our minds on the question of which plants we actually want to grow.

If our gardening career so far has shown us to be the victims of chance, luck, and serendipity, what could we now achieve, given a little focusing of the mind, a little concentration of our critical faculties, or a little forward planning? When our first garden was young and new, there seemed no need to be firm and refuse a plant that had been kindly given, or to reject a shrub seen for sale at a knockdown price. It is only later on that one learns that being more selective might have been a better course of action. But that's how it usually is in life: you have to make all your important decisions before you have the wisdom or experience to equip you for making the choices you face.

Experienced gardeners who come to make a second or a third garden have a significant advantage over their younger selves. Instead of going by instinct, or saying "I like the look of that", they can select their plants on the basis of past experience. In most spheres of endeavour it makes sense to know the material you are working with before setting out

BELOW A border themed in pastel shades at Coughton Court in Warwickshire. With their soft, rounded outlines, most of these plants would come into the "fillers" category.

like your own, or, best of all, have spent a few years growing them yourself, all this builds up into an invaluable resource.

SELECTIVE OR ECLECTIC

For some people, the idea of sitting down soberly and planning out the entire garden with lists and diagrams may feel too calculating—surely, this will take all the fun out of it? Armed with all the plant catalogues, plant encyclopedias, and other plant references that sit on the shelves, how can anyone begin to make a shortlist? But to have a strategy is likely to produce better results than simply juggling with what is to hand. There is pleasure to be gained from plants acquired by chance, it is true, but to move beyond serendipity is probably what we need to give us the outcome we want. Being ruthless and hard-headed might pay off in the end.

Assuming a reasonable level of plant knowledge, the experienced gardener will have acquired enough humility by now to realize that some decisions have already been made about the new plot. The site will have its own individual characteristics and limitations. It may have limy soil, it may be near the coast, or it may have winter temperatures that will restrict the choices that can be made; all these are among life's great unalterables. Those years of gardening experience will have taught us that "experimenting" with tender plants, or dabbling with lime-haters or any other unsuitable material will only end in tears, and if we try to defy the laws of nature, time and effort is simply wasted. When we accept the limitations of the site there will still be plenty of choice to meet the demands of climate, soil, and ecology.

on a project. We expect a carpenter to know how to work with wood, and a painter to know his paint before he begins his picture. So to know your plants is a huge advantage, and if you have visited successful gardens open to view and seen plants growing in the gardens of the great and good, if you've been to the gardens of enthusiasts who have smaller plots

One policy in a new garden is simply to pick "the best of everything". This what the term "eclectic collection" implies, but what is "the best of everything"? Supposing a garden is owned by a couple and both are plant enthusiasts—a common occurrence—would they ever agree on the subject? On its own, "the best of everything" is probably too vague and controversial a strategy. So, are there any other traditional starting points we can employ? One tried and tested approach to planting schemes is colour. It certainly seems tempting to focus on those alluring highlights of the garden, the flowers. However, while flowers are undeniably beautiful, they are not everything. Flowers come and go, but the plant as a whole carries on, and one has to ask what the plant as a whole contributes to the garden. For example, one of my gardening friends won't grow roses. Their flowers may be wonderful, she says, but on balance, bearing in mind what a typical rose bush looks like from September to May (that is, for most of the year) she thinks a rose bush is too ugly to have a place in her garden. You and I may not agree with her, but you can see her point.

MAKING AN IMPACT

So instead of dividing plants into those that have pink flowers, those that have white, and so on, there may be a more useful method of putting plants into

BELOW However
attractive and unusual a
Sempervivum may be, it will
be too small to make any
impact on the garden as a
whole. Nice when seen close
to, but not big enough to
have any effect on the
general garden picture.

BELOW Pointed conifers
make a major statement in
the garden—their shape
even resembles an
exclamation mark. If they
also have coloured foliage,
then this feature increases
their dominant effect.

categories. A good way of thinking about plants is to consider what effect they have in the garden. I call it their Impact Rating. Plants are like people—some have strong characters and others are more easy-going. Some plants make a major visual impression; others are quiet little do-gooders, attractive close to, but not attracting much attention to themselves from a distance. A yucca, for example, makes an extremely strong statement, its sharply pointed leaves suggesting that you should stand back to admire it. At the other extreme a low-growing, low-impact cranesbill geranium such as *Geranium asphodeloides* is fairly reticent. About six inches (15 cm) high, it will give you a succession of pleasing flowers over a period of many weeks, but the plant as a whole has no consistent shape or discernible outline; it simply spills out like pale pink icing to fill the space available, spreading quietly (but not aggressively) along the surface of the ground until it meets another plant. In this way, its size and shape are determined by the plants that adjoin it. So *Geranium asphodeloides* is a blender, an accommodating fitter-in, whose only aim is to please.

Rather than colour, season, or floral beauty, impact is in many ways a more helpful way to discriminate between plants and organize the garden. In any planting scheme we need to know which are the major players, and which the minor characters, the subordinates, the plants playing a supporting role. Size necessarily counts when it comes to impact. They may all be interesting, looked at one by one, but some you will be able to see from the living room window, and some you won't. A pointed conifer six feet (2 m) tall will stand out like a bold exclamation mark, whereas its dwarf counterpart—*Thuja occidentalis* 'Danica', for example—will also make a statement, but a lesser one, acting more like a semi-colon or a comma. Sempervivums in a court-yard outside the dining room window are fine, but from a distance it will make no difference whether you planted sempervivums or sprinkled grey gravel, the effect will be the same. This is an issue of scale, in the sense that a plant needs to match its context. Gunnera would look coarse and almost grotesque in a small suburban garden, because of its sheer size and rough texture, but beside a large lake it looks fine. To take a more extreme example, a Wellingtonia (*Sequoiadendron giganteum*) will dwarf almost any-thing: in most town or suburban gardens it would simply be a case of either having the tree, or having a garden—you couldn't have both. At the other extreme, a little flowering cherry would look lost on the edge of a sports field, but will be perfect in the average back garden. Large trees are for large-scale landscapes; tiny plants are for tiny places.

Form also contributes a great deal to a plant's impact. Most conifers have a very distinct outline or silhouette, in contrast with the average perennial, which is soft and vaguely rounded. Deciduous flower-ing shrubs cover themselves with flowers, but have no particular shape. This is not necessarily a dis-advantage, since a garden cannot be filled with

strong shapes: the result would be too congested and chaotic, like the competing individualistic skyscrapers of many modern cities.

COLOUR AND IMPACT

After size and shape, intensity of colour is another factor affecting the impact of a plant. *Kniphofia*

uvaria, for instance, with its brilliant orangy red-hot poker flowerheads, will inevitably have greater impact than a plant that has pastel flowers—the washed-out pink spires of *Sidalcea* 'Elsie Heugh', for example, or the pale spikes of *Lysimachia ephemerum*. The same applies to the colour of foliage. A walk through a rhododendron and azalea garden out of season soon demonstrates the gloom and heaviness of the dark foliage of the rhododendrons, compared with the "lightness of being" of the pale green leaves of the deciduous azaleas.

Purple foliage is particularly problematic. The gloom and darkness of a purple-leaved tree stands out very obviously among "normal", green-leaved

people's gardens. If I were forced to choose a large dark-leaved shrub I would prefer one of the varieties of *Sambucus nigra*, which are not quite so heavy and intense in their colour.

The problem with purple-leaved plants of small proportions is quite the reverse: instead of being too obtrusive, they tend to disappear altogether from view. From a distance they seem to produce a dark hole in the bed. The subtle nuances of the purple markings on the leaves of a dark-leaved heuchera can be easily appreciated when you are within arm's length of the plant, but from any farther away than that the effect is non-existent.

DOMINANT AND SUB-DOMINANT

To consider the "impact rating" of plants is particularly useful when first thinking about a new planting scheme. It is best to take the strong-charactered plants first and decide where they should be placed; when that is done, less dominant plants can be placed between them. Of course you don't need to

trees, an effect that is not that pleasant to my way of thinking, especially in a rural setting. In my view, any plant more than two feet (60 cm) high looks better with green leaves than it does in purple form. Some people enthuse over *Cercis canadensis* 'Forest Pansy', but I am very happy to admire it in other

OPPOSITE TOP The strong and the weak: a group of vertically shaped evergreens combine with some soft and "frothy" planting to create a pleasing overall effect.

OPPOSITE BOTTOM This planting has attractive colours, but because it has been designed as a "meadow" it deliberately lacks any high-impact plants.

BELOW With its long flowering period, *Erysimum* 'John Codrington' makes an excellent choice as a "filler" plant in the garden.

have any dominant plants at all, if that is the effect that you want. In his gardens, the designer Percy Cane often used huge swathes of deciduous azaleas, enjoying the consistency of their rounded, arching shape. But if suddenly a plant with stronger impact is used, it should not be allowed just to "creep into" the scheme of things in some chance location. It has to be placed in a spot where impact and emphasis are appropriate.

With perennials, all-low-impact plantings are less likely to work. Endless use of cranesbill geraniums in a garden is a recipe for tedium unless you break their fluffy, formless "froth" with something tougher and more definite. In such a context, a dome-shaped shrub such as clipped box, a small hebe, or a dwarf berberis would provide a welcome break. From perennials one might choose something much more dramatic, such as an *Acanthus mollis*, an ornamental grass, or a plant with vertical flower spikes. Alternatively one could contrast all that floral "fluff" with the bold foliage of bergenias or of Corsican hellebores (*Helleborus argutifolius*).

DELICIOUS FILLINGS

It would be wrong to imagine that high-impact plants are somehow superior to low-impact ones. Both are needed, and successful planting schemes are usually a blend of high-impact plants and others, which are sometimes called "fillers". Needless to say, many fillers are very beautiful; they just don't shout as loudly as their high-impact neighbours. Cranesbill geraniums (all that "froth") make perfect fillers, as do alchemillas, gypsophila, lamb's ears (*Stachys*), and a whole range of worthwhile ground coverers.

How to choose our fillers? Usually we pick them up by chance over the course of the years, but anyone making a new garden or a new border has the chance to adopt a more considered approach. First of all, we could look out for plants that bloom for a long period of time, since these will give us good value for money. Second, we could choose ground-cover plants, since these will cut down on the need to weed. And thirdly, we could decide that we want a succession of colour and interest throughout the year. We want to go out there every day of the year and find new things happening.

So in the first category—plants that flower for a long period—we could choose perennial wallflowers such as *Erysimum* 'Bowles' Mauve' or *E.* 'John Codrington', or euphorbias such as *E. cyparissias*, which will give weeks of colour—bright yellow, later fading to apricot. This euphorbia runs about, so don't plant it among rarities on the rock garden, but in front of shrubs or between tough things like peonies or daylilies. Later on we could have some of

the wonderful hardy fuchsias, which will flower right up until the first frosts arrive.

Among the excellent range of plants that can be grown as ground cover (which is our second category of fillers) we might well select some of the cranesbill geraniums, and there are several good low-growing varieties such as 'Little Gem', 'Orkney Pink'. and *G. renardii*, which has greyish, rounded leaves, not typical of a geranium. Margery Fish once said that she had one rule in gardening: "when in doubt, plant *Geranium endressii*." Although quite common in gardens, it is very reliable, and its foliage overwinters for me. If you choose a selected form, or a near hybrid, such as *G.* × *oxonianum* 'Wargrave Pink', you will find that the (many) seedlings will vary slightly in colour, giving a "multi" effect. The lovely *G.* 'Mary Mottram' looks as if it is a good white

form of *G. endressii. Geranium versicolor album* has a longer, if less dramatic display, and is nearly as good. There are also several good cultivated varieties of *G. sylvaticum*, such as 'Amy Doncaster', 'Mayflower', and 'Birch Lilac'. Ground cover does not have be ivy, lamiums, or hypericum. It can be something much more floriferous, as later chapters on perennials will explore.

Colour and change during the course of the year can be provided by our third category of fillers, and to describe this at any length would be to write another book. Part of the pleasure of gardening is to be able to go around the garden and see what is coming up, what is coming into flower, and what is dying down. Beginning with snowdrops, winter-flowering heathers, hellebores, and spring bulbs, we move on later into spring with euphorbias, irises, and a whole range of flowering shrubs. Then come the rhododendrons and azaleas, roses, clematis, and, as high summer comes, a whole array of perennials—a multitude too vast to enumerate. Finally come the Michaelmas daisies and the other richly coloured members of the genus *Aster*, along with Japanese anemones, followed by chrysanthemums, and then the pleasures of berries and autumn foliage as the year draws to a close.

HALFWAY HOUSES

But to divide plants into two camps—the strong and the weak—is to create a false dichotomy, since these are simply two extremes, and in between lies a whole range of plants of intermediate impact. Some plants are strong characters when they are up and running in the appropriate season, but have little

impact for the rest of the year. Many of the large perennials make a major statement, but only for a month or so, such as the large actaeas (formerly *Cimicifuga*), *Echinops* (globe thistles), thalictrums, kniphofias, and *Cardiocrinum giganteum*. After that they have to be cut down, and after lying dormant all winter it takes them all summer to get back up to their full height again. Similarly *Eremurus* are most dramatic when in flower, but this is only for a week or so at the most.

Foliage plants represent another intermediate position. Bold foliage plants come in a "fairly dominant" category, with a rating of six, seven, or eight marks out of ten for impact. Among shrubs, the winners are perhaps the mahonias, although I also admire *Fatsia japonica*. Among perennials, the foliage qualities of hostas are well-known to gardeners, but there are many other attractive possibilities, such as rodgersias, bergenias, *Darmera peltata* (for the waterside), the Corsican hellebore, and ornamental rhubarbs (*Rheum*).

Coloured foliage can also be used to create a moderate amount of garden impact, but a little care is needed here. Silver foliage looks wonderful with white and blue flowers seen on a sunny day. But deprived of the sunshine factor, quite a few of the silver-leaved plants look quite drab and miserable—*Artemisia alba* 'Canescens', for instance, looks particularly dismal in the winter. Plants with purple and brown foliage have their devotees. More exciting is blue foliage. The blue hostas are much admired plants; the blue grass *Leymus arenarius* also has its attractions, and the glaucous *Crambe maritima* (sea cabbage) is unlike most other plants in the garden. But one point to bear in mind with blue hostas is that they say "Horticulture" very loudly indeed—in other words, they look very cultivated. Blue hostas planted out in a naturalistic woodland planting can look rather incongruous.

There are many splendid gold- or yellow-leaved plants falling in this "medium-impact" category— the dwarf bamboo *Pleioblastus viridistriatus* (syn. *P. auricomus*), for instance, or *Carex elata* 'Aurea' (Bowles' golden sedge). Even yellow privet is not to be despised, especially if given space to grow gracefully instead of being clipped into miserable lumps.

But the same comment in regard to blue hostas applies equally to Bowles' golden sedge—that brilliant splash of yellow makes it a garden plant, not a wild one. Good variegated plants are also almost too numerous to name—among shrubs there are excellent forms of *Cornus*, weigela, and holly, and dwarf variegated euonymus is indispensable for brightening

up dark shady corners. Among perennials plants I particularly like the variegated spikes of *Iris pallida* 'Variegata', and recently I "discovered" the umbelliferous *Peucedanum ostruthium* 'Daphnis', like an improved relation of variegated ground elder, only taller and better-behaved. There are many variegated grasses: *Miscanthus* cultivars are among the most sensational. *Vinca major* 'Variegata' is an essential filler for those difficult shady areas.

These various kinds of coloured foliage do not necessarily look good together. To plant the blue *Hosta* 'June' next to the red-tinted leaves of rodgersia is passable, but to add yellow *Filipendula ulmaria* 'Aurea' would be overdoing it. The three rules when it comes to using coloured foliage plants are moderation, moderation, and moderation.

Another interesting foliage effect that some plants have is good texture, and this, too, contributes to their impact in the garden. *Colutea arborescens* (bladder senna) is a study in fine, delicate sea-green. The leaves of *Viburnum rhytidophyllum* are large and leathery. Many limoniums are a mass of fine featheriness which contrasts interestingly with some of the bold-leaved plants discussed above.

PLANTS AS PERSONALITIES

What is presented in this chapter is a way of looking at plants. No-one can tell the enthusiast exactly what to plant—one person loves daphnes and the next loves *Digitalis*; one looks down on dahlias, while another hates arisaemas. But to view the vast selection of plants available as if they were different personality types can be useful when placing plants together in the garden. Forget the detail of purple mottling at the base of the petals, or any other minor charm—it's much more useful to consider the overall impact of the plant. So if someone has a special interest in alchemillas, acaenas, epimediums, *Omphalodes*, *Paris*, or *Vancouveria*, they obviously have a predilection for quiet types—low-impact plants—attractive in themselves but not dramatic in the garden. Something else will be needed to liven up the places where such perennials are grown—a few plants with greater impact that will prevent the border looking uninteresting from a distance. On the other hand, if the garden owner has a passion for phormiums, South American eryngiums, and agaves, there will be a call not only for protective clothing, but also for some calmer, less ferocious plants to pour oil on the water between those strong characters, and make the border look a less hectic and more balanced affair.

4
The single-genus collection

ANYONE WHO WANTS to make a single-genus plant collection today has a great deal of help at hand, in terms of the information available. In Britain, Australia, New Zealand, and some North American regions there are the *Plant Finder* publications, which enable the vital question of the availability of plants to be answered at a glance. In addition, the internet gives immediate access to a huge number of colour-illustrated nursery catalogues, as well as fact-files, botanical databases and so on, providing a vast, chaotic, and kaleidoscopic array of material.

However, more important than information is the initial spark of interest that sets you going in the first place. After that, the next requirement is a modicum of dedication to follow it through. Determination and persistence will need to be among your personality traits, since you will have to focus your attention on something for several years at a stretch, and you also need a reasonable amount of time to dedicate to your interest. In my own case, my enthusiasm suffered a dip after a few years, and collecting euphorbias then became for me a textual, or paper exercise—resulting in a book rather than a living plant collection. Space is needed, not only for growing the mature plants, but also for trialling new ones, bringing on seedlings, and taking cuttings, and the fact was that I wanted to grow other plants in my garden besides euphorbias.

ON THE EUPHORBIA TRAIL
The abundance of information available today makes setting out to collect plants of one particular type a significantly different experience from my

own. When I began to collect euphorbias, in the mid-1970s, I naturally started by consulting a large number of reference books, although the number of volumes of encyclopedic proportions available then was far smaller than it is today. There was no way of telling then exactly how many euphorbias were in cultivation. You had to write directly to the nurseries you thought were likely to stock them and ask them to send you their catalogues. You had to put your ear to the ground, you wrote to the authors of books, consulted the grapevine, and generally put out the word.

Luck, the generosity of others, and personal contacts all helped. Soon after setting out on my quest, I joined the Hardy Plant Society, and publicized the fact that I was looking for euphorbias in the pages of its newsletter. This introduced me to many people with hearts of gold, who gave me plants and pointed me in useful directions.

I particularly remember the day (long before various motorways were built) when we made a trip to meet the late John Raven, classics scholar and author of *The Botanist's Garden*, who showed me the euphorbias in his garden and then took me to the edge of a seemingly random Cambridgeshire wheat field, where we dug up a small piece of *Euphorbia × pseudovirgata*—a plant that farmers view as an unpleasant weed.

I wrote to all the major gardens in the country, both botanic and otherwise, and asked them which euphorbias they grew. I met the euphorbia expert at Kew, Alan Radcliffe-Smith, who answered my long letters and was generally very patient. He also gave me seeds that had been sent to Kew Gardens from the

Middle East several years earlier by a plant-hunting botanist. They had not been tried at Kew for various reasons—euphorbias were apparently not considered important enough to take up valuable staff time and/or space on the ground (how Kew could be short of space I could never understand). But sadly these seeds were several years old, and not many of them germinated.

Somehow I got hold of an international list of botanic gardens and sent off more letters. In those days, if you appeared serious enough, the botanic gardens of the USSR and Eastern Europe would send you their seed lists without asking any questions, and then give you seeds of rare euphorbias (and anything else you asked for) free of charge. I do hope these wonderful institutions still exist.

BELOW LEFT Comparing the bark of various unusual birches: *Betula albosinensis* var. *septentrionalis*.

BELOW RIGHT *Betula utilis* at Stone Lane Gardens, Devon. This particular tree was grown from seed from Sichuan, in China.

Of course, discovering which nursery offers a plant is not the same thing as acquiring it. Take the case of *Euphorbia* × *martini* 'Red Dwarf', which I found to be a most worthwhile plant when I eventually saw it, some time after I had written about it in my book. It was first discovered in the garden of Richard and Janet Blenkinship, who used to run a nursery in Lincolnshire, but they sold plants only at the nursery—no mail order was offered. From my home in Gloucestershire to Lincolnshire may be only a few hours' drive, but somehow I never found myself travelling in that direction until sometime in the late 1990s—by which time the Blenkinships had sold their nursery, and on the day I telephoned, the new owner was unsure whether she had any plants or not. So it was some time before I acquired this excellent plant. But even as I write today, none of the five small nurseries in Britain that allegedly offer this euphorbia have put their plant lists on the internet, although one does have a website. Having a collection can well mean finding the time and making the effort to drive some distance to get your hands on plants that you lack.

A SERIOUS BUSINESS

There's a lot of pleasure in finding and acquiring a species or cultivar that's new to you, especially when it is a rare one. You look at your little baby sitting snugly in your garden, knowing that it could well be that nobody else in the country (possibly in the world) is growing it. Comparing one species with another is useful and interesting, as is comparing plants from different sources. Will a plant grown from seed collected from the wild on the mountains

of Honshu (or wherever it might be) look anything like the plant of the same name bought from a local nursery, where it has been "bred in captivity" for generations? The result may be better, or it may be worse! Then there is the "odd" seedling that is different from all the rest. Is it just odd, or is it a major improvement on the usual form grown? Dare you name it?

A moderate amount of efficiency is required if you want to pursue this interest seriously. This is needed in simple but neverthless vital matters, such as not losing the labels of plants. The same applies to the names of seeds, and making sure that the labels on pots of seedlings are firmly attached. Having taken the trouble to raise a rare plant, it's annoying for everybody if, at the end of the day, nobody knows for certain what it is. If it was collected on a distant mountainside as "*Haplopappus* sp." that's

plants clearly and correctly labelled. If the garden is only open on request, or on only one day a year, it's forgivable if the owners have to retrieve the label from under the foliage for their guests, but once you are into regular unaccompanied openings, then clear, bold labels are an essential part of the business. Getting involved in letting people see your collection is inevitably an exercise in information-sharing, and although easily read labels are intrusive, they're indispensable for the garden visitor. "Nice *Rhodohypoxis*, but which is it?" could be the comment from the devotee who has driven a long way to see your collection. In some cases, it may be necessary to provide the visitor with help in actually finding the plants in the garden. You know where they are, but in a large garden, it may not be at all obvious. Little maps or guides may be a bore, but the weary traveller who comes from somewhere distant to see your rare *Askidiosperma* collection will be upset if he later discovers that he missed another whole bed of them tucked behind the greenhouse.

Keeping paper records is also important. I was forced to distribute some euphorbias as Leningrad 1077, 1078, and 1079, because I mislaid the seed list from Leningrad (now St Petersburg) Botanic Garden, where the seeds had come from. Little inefficiencies like this can be embarrassing later on.

Would-be collection-holders can easily be put off by imagining there is a lot of paperwork involved in having a collection. There need not be, but common sense does apply. Keeping a file of correspondence, in date-order, is not that onerous. An address book is also useful, along with a date-order notebook or garden diary. Making a list of the species or cultivars

one thing, but if it's "*Haplopappus* sp." just because its name has been mislaid, that's not so good.

If the garden is open to the public, the most useful thing the collection holder can do is to have the

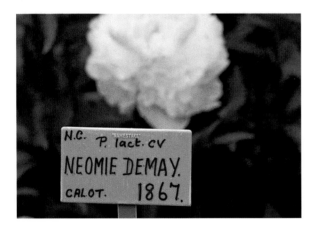

according to the books—in case it turns out to be different in reality. You can always add more information at a later stage.

A file of photocopied botanical information can be useful, if you're really keen, and a bibliography can be invaluable; after all, this is only a list of the books you've consulted on the subject. If you ever manage to get to the reference library of some learned institution, it's useful to keep a note (in your garden notebook, not on some scrappy piece of paper) of the books you looked at, or which books photocopied information came from. Obvious, but easily overlooked.

GOING PUBLIC

Anyone who goes public with their collection raises a whole new level of expectation. It is one thing to have a hundred arisaemas hidden away in the back garden as some eccentric hobby, when the only problem is how to withstand the tolerant amusement of the other adult person in the household— "Sorry, Harold can't come to the telephone right now, he's potting up his arisaemas," and other droll remarks. But it is quite another thing to let it be known that you have this Serious Collection of Botanic Importance, which keen gardeners and anyone else who is interested may visit.

Annual open days will prove not to be stress-free. As the big day approaches sleep is lost, days are taken off work, and beads of sweat appear on the forehead as the owner addresses the key question— am I and my collection looking our best? All of a sudden, presentation becomes an issue. The owner has hardly noticed that while loving care has been

that you have so far is also an obvious thing to do. Keep it simple: a straightforward word-processing document which can grow as necessary will be fine. Keep a copy on disk and on paper, in case your computer crashes. Avoid fancy spreadsheet or data-entry programmes: where you got each plant from, and when you acquired it, is all you need to make a start. To this you could add what it's supposed to look like

BELOW A plant that the author was forced to distribute as "ex Leningrad" after he lost the label. Well— we all make mistakes.

lavished on the machaerantheras (or whatever), the rest of the garden has gone to rack and ruin. There is a rush to clear away the clutter, mow the lawn, and do a bit of hasty weeding.

The owner will know which machaeranthera is which. But will the visitors? Suddenly labels are absolutely vital. The owner will know in which obscure corners of the garden to find each of the machaerantheras. But will the visitors ever find them? The owner isn't bothered that, because of the pressures of space, some of the machaerantheras are being grown between the compost heap and the refuse bins. It's too late now—the visitors will have to put up with it. The owner will know which machaeranthera is exceedingly rare, which machaeranthera is the only example in cultivation, which machaeranthera has an Award of Merit from the Royal Horticultural Society—but will the visitors? Is a Useful List required?

You might think this might put people off the whole idea of opening their gardens, and make them retreat into the lonely world of their strange hobby, as if it were a vice to be practised in private. But the fact is that to form a collection of one kind of plant is extremely rewarding, like a drug that is hard to resist, an ego-trip to be tasted again and again. Your opinion is asked. Your advice is sought. Your powers of identification are put to use. Your experience of propagation, your skill at cultivation, and your astonishing knowledge of names are all to be admired. Suddenly you have become an Expert. And what is more, you acquire powers of plant acquisition. That seedling of some rare euphorbia, rhodohypoxis, machaeranthera, arisaema or whatever, is currency to be traded for some other rarity possessed by another plant enthusiast.

Many well-known genera still lack an enthusiast to collect them, and champion their charms. Where, in Britain at least, is the collection of climbing *Lonicera*, or of Darwin tulips? It's absorbing, rewarding, and better than video games. I recommend it. Your country needs you.

5
A strategy for the garden

IT IS CLEAR THAT creating a single-genus collection has a major impact on the garden, and that comparatively few people will want to devote themselves to such a single-minded form of gardening endeavour. A general plant collection, on the other hand, is the horticultural element of any garden, and in this case a few ideas on garden-making may well be appropriate at this stage.

BROAD BRUSH VERSUS NITTY-GRITTY

Anyone who has taken on a large project will know that there is a variety of ways to tackle it. Whether the project is to make some large-scale artefact, a book, a business plan or whatever, there are two basic ways of approaching the matter, depending on which end of the telescope you prefer. One way to begin is to consider one or two of the key details or issues, resolve these, and from there one can build up the bigger picture. The second technique is to stand back at the outset, consider the problem as a whole, use a broad brush first, and sort the detail out later. Whichever way you begin there are hazards. If you start with the grand plan there may be details whose significance you have not fully appreciated, and it might turn out that these will throw the whole scheme out of kilter. On the other hand, if we start with the details, we won't necessarily know which ones to start with, or which detail has priority if one conflicts with another.

As an analogy, consider a very small project: making a flower arrangement. You might start by going out into the garden to pick whatever flowers are available. It may happen that all the flowers you find

are only six inches (15 cm) tall, but this may not matter; there is bound to be somewhere where they will look right. You then choose a suitable vase and proceed to make the arrangement. Finally you walk around the house to find a spot where it will look

BELOW This may look like a general shot of the garden, but in fact it is the boundary of a town garden, with the fence hidden by the pale yellow rambler rose 'Alister Stella Gray'.

for an event in a public hall, with Ionic columns and galleries all round. Immediately we know that a huge display will be required, and the modest blooms available in our own garden will be useless. We will have to go to the florist and buy bigger ones, and many more of them.

The first approach might be called making use of the resources available. The second was an exercise in problem-solving. When making a garden, both ways of looking at the project are needed. We need to move back and forth between the detail and the whole, to consider both the individual plants and the question of what kind of garden we want. Nearly every plant enthusiast has stood in the middle of the lawn with a plant in their hands, wondering where it should go. At some stage we need to look through the other end of the telescope, and think about what kind of plants the garden needs, and what sort of garden we want.

First of all we have to accept our limitations. How much scope do we have? In all probability we are not making a Kew or a Versailles, but turning a very small plot into a place where we can grow plants and enjoy some outdoor living. The scope for achieving a very wide range of aims will, therefore, be limited. In fact, there will probably be space only to do one thing well, and one or two simple effects will be all that is needed for a successful outcome. Some shrubs, a pebble garden, a bit of decking, a Lutyens-style seat, a bright blue vase, a few roses, a collection of pulmonarias, a few rows of assorted vegetables and the remnants of a lawn (much bitten into and depleted)—all this would be impossible to bring together into a pleasing whole. Instead we

good. But to approach the task from the "opposite end" would be to know from the start where the arrangement is to stand, and what function it must serve. It may be for a wedding, to stand at the front of a chapel or church—or perhaps the flowers are

need to concentrate our minds and decide on what type of garden it is to be, and what are the most important aims we want to achieve.

Large gardens can offer even greater temptations than small ones. In fact, just as much concentration of effort is needed in very large gardens, for success will elude us if we allow too many aims and aspirations to complicate the issue. One issue that needs deliberate thought in gardens visited by the public is the question of routes through the garden. After visiting some large gardens, one comes away remarking that there were wonderful plants, but when it comes to finding your way around, "confusion here hath made her masterpiece".

APPROPRIATE BEHAVIOUR

Those of us who have town or suburban gardens are inevitably blessed with views of other people's houses, walls, fences, the garage, and neighbouring gardens. Necessarily any thoughts of prairie or meadow gardens, lime-tree avenues, woodland gardens, and arboreta have to be put aside as non-starters in a small-scale environment that is obviously man-made. In a rural situation, on the other hand, the local landscape may be visible over the fence, and it will be necessary to acknowledge its character in the garden. A garden among orchards or gentle, cultivated farmland will need to look different from one high up on a stretch of wild moorland, and if we try to ignore this factor we may create something that looks incongruous in its setting.

The scale of the house will suggest the scale of the garden. Grand houses, for example, need grand gardens; cottage gardens are for cottages. However, most of us live in average houses, with average possibilities. The architectural style of the house can also suggest an appropriate response, including the use of sympathetic materials. But again, many houses are stylistically rather bland, which at least gives the garden-maker plenty of scope. The formal garden, which is an obsession with some, seems to me to require a formal house, and a relationship between house and garden. Tudor gardens are fine in front of Tudor houses, but to turn a corner on some winding grass path and suddenly come across an exercise in formality detached from anything else (as one sometimes sees) makes very little sense.

Similarly, any attempt to transport the Japanese garden into western suburbia is fraught with problems. The culture gap is bigger than you think. The Japanese style looks great in photographs, but those of us who are used to English-style gardens may find there is something lacking. With less herbaceous material, the garden doesn't respond to the seasons in the same way, and also the scale is wholly different:

TOP RIGHT Screening things we don't want to see may be one of the first tasks in garden-making. This screen is in a small town garden designed the author.

BOTTOM RIGHT Old walls can be a mixed blessing—if the bricks are a harsh orange-red, for example, they may clash with the flower colour. The plants here are *Lysimachia clethroides* and *Erysimum* 'Bowles' Mauve'.

you must tiptoe (in a kimono, in Japanese shoes), slowly, slowly appreciating each delicate nuance as you go. The mixture of confident strides and sudden stops to look at a plant that most of us are used to is wrong for Japanese gardens. Nor can you mix the Japanese garden with anything else. You cannot have a Japanese garden *and* a few rose bushes. A Japanese garden has to be absolutely itself.

If there are certain plants that you are determined to grow, you must have the right garden to contain them. It's no good having a passion for rhododendrons if you live in a limestone or chalky-soiled area. An obsession with growing large trees cannot be catered for in town. Alpines are obviously small enough to suit the tiniest garden, but there can be dangers in having an excess of alpines. If there is nothing in the garden over six inches (15 cm) high it will look odd, and the view from the windows of the house may well be of the fence at the far end.

A ROOM WITH A VIEW

Where do we begin to make a strategic plan for the garden? One simple starting point is the view from the windows of the house. What do we see? Do we like what we see? What is revealed by that aid to uncompromising realism—the viewfinder of a camera? First of all there may be some blot on the landscape that needs screening—someone else's shed, our own vegetable plot, or the neighbour's washing line. Nothing will look any good until that intrusion has been dealt with. A hedge or a cleverly placed tree may be the answer, large enough, but not so large that its shade and hungry roots will eventually cause problems. Alternatively, if we are too impatient to

wait for a tree to grow, and if the object that needs to be hidden is not too tall, a constructed screen may be appropriate. Climbing plants can then be grown over it to soften its outline.

Even if there are no obtrusive buildings or other objects that need to be hidden, the boundaries of the plot may still not be all that attractive, and dealing with this will be our next task. Not even the nicest old wall or artistically designed fence is as restful to the eye as leaves and greenery. Fences and walls have

a way of emphasizing the straight edges of a plot, and also reminding us of the limitations of its size. Phase One of any scheme to improve the garden will include a decision to plant an interesting range of climbers and wall shrubs around the perimeter of the garden, to clothe the boundaries.

FORM AND FUNCTION

Practical considerations must be included in the overall strategy. Even the most fanatical gardener

will want to sit down occasionally, and someone has to decide where this should be. Although one can put chairs out on the lawn in the summer, a paved terrace is more useful. It could be immediately outside the house, further down the garden in a suntrap, or in the shade of an old apple tree—only the garden owners can decide where it should be, but it needs to be treated as one of the most important parts of the overall scheme. It will be from here that you will sit and enjoy the view of the garden.

A working area will also be needed for a shed or storage area, perhaps a greenhouse or plastic tunnel, and compost heaps. Most keen plantspeople are also keen propagators, and space will be needed for potting up, and keeping pots of seedlings, cuttings, and young plants. All this can be of consuming interest to the mind, but is unlikely to be of beauty to the eye. The usual solution is to give it its own separate compartment, screened from the rest of the garden.

LAWN AND ORDER

Plants, borders, lawn, seating area, paths, working areas, beds—how can we find a framework into which all these parts can fit? We need a hook, as it were, to hang everything on. One could take a leaf from the book of the modern museum designer, who plans the routes around the galleries and internal spaces as carefully as the display of the collection itself, knowing that to guide the visitors—to pause here, to move along there—will greatly enhance their experience of the visit.

Displaying plants is a similar exercise. One of the best ways of creating a framework for the garden consists of looking carefully at the spaces, places

where you stand, places where there are no plants. In other words, it's the lawn, the paths, and the paved areas that give us the key to laying out the garden, rather than the plants. Like a display area in a museum, the lawn can be thought of as a room in which plants (as opposed to interesting objects) can be seen to advantage. The lawn, like a room, should have a shape of its own, a logical and simple shape, as rooms usually do. On no account should the lawn be quietly forgotten, or thought of as what is left over

after the borders have been made. Simplicity and clarity are virtues when it comes to making rooms, and the same approach applies to lawns. Squares or rectangles are not boring shapes, but sensible, rational ones, as suitable for lawns as they are for rooms. If there are any irregular, "left-over" spaces, let them be in the borders, which can be planted up: their irregularity will not show once they are full of plants, whereas the shape of the lawn is apparent for everyone to see. To introduce an arbitrary wiggle to the edge of the grass is pointless.

Because the shapes of plants are irregular and diverse, to create a lawn with a strong and clear outline is an excellent way to bring order. Of course there are many shapes that can be used for a lawn: circles, ovals, oblongs, or maybe some interesting curvaceous design, as long as it has been thought about in a rational way, and is not just some left-over grass with bites taken out of it, and random beds dropped into it. An effective way to give interest to a long or narrow lawn is to allow it to curve gently as you look down its length, in a shallow S-shape,

BELOW The *Hemerocallis*
collection at Apple Court,
near Lymington, in
Hampshire. The assembled
daylilies form a rather
shapeless mass, but the
dwarf box hedges help
by providing a neat
evergreen finish to the
edge of the border.

but always keeping the width constant, like a green highway with the curves parallel on each side.

Another important aim is to make the lawn as level as possible, or at least on a level plane. A lawn that slopes sideways will always feel uncomfortable. Sloping borders might be thought of as difficult, but I have found from experience that if a sloping border is planted with shrubs or ground cover it is surprising how little the gradient shows. Some gardens slope so much that it is hard to make level lawns without introducing a daunting array of retaining walls, but one should still try to make the main lawn area level if at all possible. This is something that has to be done soon after moving in to a new garden. Get the digger in on Day One: the upheaval won't be welcome later.

FLESH AND BONES

Another way of bringing order and strategy to the garden is the so-called "flesh-and-bones" approach. Winter reveals the skeleton of the garden, much of the ephemeral "flesh" of flowering plants has faded

BELOW The gardens at
Sissinghurst Castle, Kent,
seen from the tower. This is
an example of the "flesh-
and-bones" approach,
where the lush planting is
the "flesh" and the yew
hedges and the shapes of
the spaces provide the
"bones" of the garden.

famous and successful garden, the division of labour—bones and flesh—was between the generations; here Christopher Lloyd has planted up a garden previously laid out by his father and his father's architect, Edwin Lutyens.

A man-made object in the garden can also act as a way of giving the garden a sense of order and focus. "Features" are often strong in themselves and easily attract attention. They don't necessarily have to be emphasized by excessive symmetry and framing, but this depends on the style of the garden. Formal gardens generate their own organization, but in a less formal garden, some ornamental object need not be so obviously "in your face". Sometimes a simple object can be added in quite a casual manner, simply to provide a break from endless greenery. Sculpture can look pretentious, and one grows tired of pseudo-Classical scantily-clad figures. Personally I prefer something more original, or else something very simple such as a plain, rounded terracotta vase, its colour and texture contrasting well with surrounding foliage. It shouldn't be forgotten that practical and necessary objects such as steps, pools, and seats are also man-made objects that can complement planting very effectively.

away, and the structural "bones" of the garden are revealed: the paths, steps, walls, and hedges. If there are conifers, evergreen shrubs, or little box hedges, these too will look good all the year around, and the way they are placed will provide a framework for the less permanent planting. Not everyone likes little box hedges, but they do have the advantage of providing a neat green edge to the border even in winter, when the rest of the plants are mostly over.

Sissinghurst, in Kent, provides an admirable example where a husband and wife team created the garden. Harold Nicolson laid down the main elements—the bones of the garden—in the form of the paths, the yew hedges, lawns, and borders, leaving his wife Vita Sackville-West to flesh out the borders with good plants. At Great Dixter, Sussex, in another

FOREGROUNDS, FRAMING, AND CIRCULAR ROUTES.

Once an overall scheme has been devised for the garden we can go back to the windows of the house, and to other key points in the garden, and consider how things will look. Once the "bones" are in place and planting is beginning to develop, we can try to picture the garden in our mind's eye, and perhaps

steal an idea or two from the art of photography to help us with the planting. Many people have had the experience of taking a photograph that turns out to be disappointing, whereas their more experienced friend made a better picture by moving a little to the left, to get the bough of a nearby tree into the picture—or maybe something in the foreground helped to make the picture more interesting. The same principles can be made to apply in the garden. As we look down the garden, or look from any significant position in the garden, the view can be framed, and

this can have an enhancing effect. It doesn't have to be done by building an archway or by planting a pair of pointed conifers, although these are common ways of achieving framing. Maybe there is simply an opening in a hedge, or a gateway of some kind. Or the framing can be more informal, perhaps between the stems of birches—the options are many. Nor does the framing idea apply just to vertical elements: views across a foreground of plants can be more interesting than simply across a plain lawn.

It is also important to look and see what there is to be seen through the frame. Any opening from one part of the garden into another will create a frame, and we need to stand back and check what we can see. Does the view make sense? Do we see something through the frame that we want to see, or is there some blot on the landscape?

Another useful rule, particularly relevant to the large garden, is to have one main route around the garden, a clearly laid out path that takes in all its major features along its route. Other minor diversions can be seen as subordinate to this main highway. The classic example of this is Stourhead in Wiltshire, admittedly on a huge scale. There are no choices to be made, or hardly any; you simply follow the path around the lake, and in this way you see the whole thing. But this philosophy can be applied on a much smaller scale. To be able to enjoy each part of the garden in turn, by going around it in the form of a circular tour, seems like common sense.

2

Collecting Garden Plants

6
Selecting trees

FOR THOSE OF US who have gardens of modest size, two or three trees, perhaps four, is the most we can expect to fit into the space available. We have to be content to choose those that are appropriate in size and performance to the garden. We may dream of all the trees that we would like to grow, but lacking places to put them, we will have to enjoy our trees in other people's gardens, in public gardens, or in an arboretum. Even so, it is worth thinking about the character and habit of the few trees that we do have, since they will be major players on our small stages. And for those gardeners who have no shortage of space, we will consider the pleasures (as well as the hazards) of bringing together a tree collection, along with the particular features and characteristics of trees of various kinds—deciduous, coniferous, or broadleaved evergreen.

THE SINGLE-GENUS COLLECTION

Even when the collector decides on a genus of small-ish trees, numbers will be the main problem facing anyone who wants to make a single-genus collection. *Crataegus*, for example, are small as trees go, but the genus does contain between 100 and 200 species (depending on which botanist you follow), of which about 60 are commercially available. The genus *Sorbus* is even larger, with about 100 species, although when subspecies, varieties, and cultivars are taken into account the total is nearer 250. So altogether this is not a project for the faint-hearted. When we come to *Prunus* and *Malus* the numbers begin to verge on the astronomic, and any would-be collector will probably decide to concentrate only on species of a particular subgenus, or maybe varieties of a

particular species. When looking at medium-sized trees, a mere five members of *Halesia*, or even 15 kinds of *Cercis*, might seem more within the realms of the possible, but with *Alnus*, *Betula*, or *Pyrus*, the numbers factor once more makes a collection a daunting enterprise. With large trees the scale of the task increases again, although naturally numbers

BELOW LEFT The
kaleidoscopic autumn
colours of *Cercidiphyllum
japonicum* take on a
translucent quality when
backlit by low afternoon
sunlight.

BELOW RIGHT A pine
tree for the tree lover's
Wants List: the elegant
needles of *Pinus
engelmannii*.

vary from genus to genus. One can't help feeling that you would need to be very dedicated indeed to want to collect 465 poplars, 260 willows, or 230 oak trees. Just to accommodate 11 kinds of plane tree requires not a garden, but grounds of several acres, and would be beyond most of us. To provide homes for a mere nine zelkovas might not be what we actu-

ally want to do with our lives or our resources—to say nothing of 45 lime trees, 42 walnuts, 65 ash trees, or 85 beeches. These all require large estates to accommodate them and an equally substantial outlay of time, money, and enthusiasm.

Sadly, the two genera that might tempt me into tree collecting (when I acquire my vast estate—and the income to manage it) are both impractically large. The genus *Pinus* to my mind contains the most wonderful trees you can find. Pines have such atmosphere: they have the power to transport you to the lands where they grow, whether on a rugged mountain top or overlooking some wonderful Italian lake. Many of the individual trees seem to be such characters in themselves, and like me, the older they get the more quirky and eccentric they become. I used to think that *Pinus pinea* was my favourite—the umbrella pine, commonly seen in Italy (there is an interesting specimen at Kew which has had to have its limbs propped up). But recently I discovered *Pinus engelmannii*, a Zone 8 American and Mexican species, which also tempts me. But regrettably there approximately 90 species of pine, and more than that number again if you count the large army of dwarf cultivars. The other genus that tempts me is *Magnolia*, but this is no better: it has 100 species and about 1,000 cultivated varieties. Ah well—in another lifetime, perhaps.

However, be not discouraged: there is a way out. Some genera only contain one species, so provided that our gardens can accommodate one tree, we can all be genus-collection-holders. I was at one time the proud owner of a collection of one *Kalopanax* (sadly, it died after a few years, for no apparent reason). *Cercidiphyllum*, *Davidia*, *Eucommia*, *Ginkgo*, *Idesia*, *Mespilus*, *Oxydendron*, *Parrotia*, and *Tetracentron* are also all interesting and monotypic. But before we smile at the absurdity of a collection of one tree, it's worth remembering that some of these single species, such as *Mespilus*, do have a handful of varieties on offer.

With some genera, climate can be a limiting factor. For example, there may only be one or two species suitable for the temperate garden, while the rest belong to the tropics or subtropics. Of 475 members of the genus *Diospyros*, only *D. kaki*, sometimes called the Chinese persimmon, is likely to be seen in frost-prone gardens (although *D. lotus*, the date plum, and *D. virginiana*, the North American persimmon, are also hardy, but possibly less ornamental). Similarly only a handful of the 1,200 *Acacia*, 800 *Ficus*, and 250 *Zanthoxylum* species can be grown outside tropical and subtropical zones. In other cases, only one or two members of a genus are normally seen in cultivation, although many more exist in the wild. Many more *Styrax* species exist in the wild than are found in garden cultivation, for example, and the same is true of *Amelanchier*, *Catalpa*, *Paulownia*, *Ptelea*, *Pterocarya*, and *Sophora*. Of course, this could be because the other species have been tried in the past and have not been found to be very attractive.

DECIDUOUS AND BROAD-LEAFED EVERGREEN TREES

Anyone making a single-genus collection of broad-leaved, deciduous trees would have little difficulty in arranging them in a pleasing manner. Those genera that consist mainly of small trees are particularly easy to plant out in an attractive way, whether in the garden or in an arboretum. *Prunus*, *Sorbus*, *Malus*, and *Crataegus*, for instance, present few problems from a visual point of view. They are rounded in shape and blend well with each other, or with other deciduous trees, and the same is true of many other genera such as *Cercis*, *Corylus*, *Cydonia*, *Halesia*, *Laburnum*, or tree-sized *Cornus* species.

From the point of view of the appearance of such a collection, the larger it becomes, the greater will be the need to introduce an element of contrast. Evergreen trees will be ideal, since they will make the collection look more attractive during the winter. Of course one can also use shrubs for this purpose, which will add a whole new layer of interest.

When it comes to the mixed planting of trees, and the question of which ones to plant with which, the same principle applies to a collection of trees in a

garden or arboretum as to a selection of perennials in a border. You need a certain amount of unity, and a certain amount of variety. This is true of the scheme as a whole, and also to any part of it. This rule may sound contradictory, since unity implies that the plants are all the same, or at least similar, while variety implies that they are all different or contrasting. However, the best results are obtained when there is enough variety to prevent boredom, but not so much that there is a restless or chaotic effect. There also needs to be enough unity to give a feeling of consistency, that this garden or arboretum is a distinct place with its own character, without it being monotonous.

In practice one can go a long way with deciduous trees before the result becomes either boring or repetitive. This is because most of us are accustomed to deciduous woodland, with its consistency and repetition of species. Native habitats normally consist of one or two types of dominant tree, usually with one or two smaller, secondary species at the woodland fringes or in openings or glades. When the number of species is limited, a pleasing sense of unity is created: it is recognizably a beech wood, say, and not a muddle of different things, and a beech wood has its own character, which anyone familiar with beech woods will instantly recognize. Each tree is likely to be of a different age, each one will have acquired a slightly different shape, and the amount of space between the trees will vary, all creating changing effects of light, shade, and colour through the year and thus providing endless variety.

A tree collection differs from a native wood because in a collection many of the trees need to be seen as individuals, so that their distinct features can be appreciated. But on the whole, deciduous, broad-leaved trees are easy-going and blend together well: from *Acer*, *Aesculus*, and *Betula* right through to *Zelkova*, what we are talking about are green, rounded, soft-outlined trees—what the British army calls fluffy-topped trees. The average soldier is not expected to be much of a tree expert, and if he or she is being given directions or making a report, only two kinds of tree are expected to be distinguished: a fir tree and a fluffy-topped tree. From our point of view, fluffy-topped trees are good mixers. They get along together very easily with other trees. One can have a group of the same species, a group of the

same genus, or a diverse group of various deciduous trees, and the effect will usually be pleasing.

Whether or not these are flowering trees makes little difference. Flowers are a temporary phenomenon, and most trees that flower are easy to place in the garden. The only tree whose flower colour is problematic is *Embothrium*, whose shade of orange clashes virulently with almost everything else in the garden or landscape, and isn't even a very pleasant shade in itself. However, as my garden is alkaline, I couldn't grow one even if I wanted to. Apart from that, a modicum of taste will suggest that it is better to keep the yellow laburnums away from the bright pink flowering cherries. Otherwise, most flowering trees, such as magnolias, cherries (*Prunus*), or crab apples (*Malus*), are very happy alongside one another. Almost all the other trees grown for their floral interest in temperate gardens have white flowers.

If the collection is large, which many single-genus collections will be, we may need to introduce a degree of variety or contrast, and this can be done by breaking up the groups with contrasting trees, such as an occasional conifer, large evergreen shrubs, or a broad-leaved evergreen tree.

Broad-leaved evergreens also fall into the easy-mixing category. Evergreen oaks, hollies, *Arbutus*, *Phillyrea latifolia*, *Ligustrum lucidum*, *Magnolia grandiflora*, *Eucalyptus*, *Chrysolepis chysophylla*, *Cotoneaster* (which occasionally reach tree size), *Eucryphia* (if you call them trees), and *Embothrium* (if you like them)—most of these are rounded, soft-edged, and "fluffy-topped", like their deciduous counterparts. One of the few conifers to fall in this rounded category is the rare and unusual *Cunninghamia lanceolata*, whose leaves are rather like those of a monkey puzzle. I have one, but it is very slow to get at all tree-like.

STRONG CHARACTERS

But some trees are more difficult to place. These are the strong-charactered trees, the high-impact plants of tree size, the ones that draw attention to themselves. Careful thought needs to be given to the positions of these in the garden or arboretum. Or more likely, one should ask whether they really should be included at all. In this group are trees with a weeping habit or abnormally upright habit, along with trees that don't have green foliage. Some books on trees take pains to list these as if they were of particular interest. What they usually omit to say is that these are the ones you should take pains to avoid, or at least use very sparingly. Some of these trees are

actually freaks of nature, and although a few of them are quite attractive, they always draw attention to themselves and say "Look at me!". One can stand a certain amount of showing off, but not too much: to contrast a fastigiate tree with a weeping tree, beyond which lurks a cedar of Lebanon, while in the foreground is a group consisting of a yellow form of Lawson cypress, a purple-leaved *Cotinus*, and a wide-spreading juniper—all this creates a riot of

disparate shapes and foliage colours, and before long we will wish it looked a bit more restful.

Sometimes one sees Lombardy poplars (*Populus nigra* 'Italica') ranged across the landscape like giant tin soldiers, but the fact is that ordinary rounded trees, as nature intended, are nicer. One weeping tree beside a lake is enough—and remember, it's been done before. It might actually be more original not to have that weeping willow or weeping ash hunched over the pond.

Among the more attractive strong-charactered trees are *Carpinus betulus* 'Fastigiata' (which I call the railway-modeller's tree) and *Robinia pseudoacacia* 'Inermis' (which ought to be called the pom-pom tree). These are not vertical, but very formal in shape. I find the robinia rather an attractive and amusing tree for a formal garden. However, upright varieties generally worth avoiding are *Fagus sylvatica* 'Dawyck' (the Dawyck beech), *Acer lobelii*, *Malus tschonoskii* and *M.* 'Van Eseltine', *Prunus* 'Spire', *Quercus robur* f. *fastigiata*, and anything else called 'Fastigiata' or 'Columnaris'. Excessively vertical varieties such as *Prunus* 'Amanogawa' and *Acer* 'Scanlon' seem to me only fit for the log pile.

Among the weeping trees, some people like *Betula pendula* 'Youngii', *Fraxinus excelsior* 'Pendula', and *Salix* × *sepulcralis* var. *chrysocoma*, and these can be used, with care. It is important to distinguish between trees where "pendulous" simply means that the ends or tips of the branches droop, which is pleasing enough, and cases where the entire branch structure seems to lack any muscle-power at all. *Betula pendula* 'Dalecarlica', *Tilia* 'Petiolaris', and *Larix decidua* are all pendulous to a degree, but not

RIGHT Strongly shaped,
pointed conifers such as
Picea omorika can be difficult
to mix with other trees,
especially if its neighbours
are equally strong characters.
Cambridge University
Botanic Garden.

too much. However, I find some weeping trees are so
weepy as to be embarrassing, and among these are
Alnus incana 'Pendula', *Cedrus atlantica* 'Glauca
Pendula', *Fagus sylvatica* 'Pendula', *Morus alba*
'Pendula', and *Prunus pendula* 'Pendula Rubra'.
Then there is the stunted Kilmarnock willow, *Salix
caprea* var. *pendula*, and the ugly Camperdown elm,
Ulmus glabra 'Camperdownii', which both make
good firewood.

Weeping and upright varieties are horticultural
trees, trees which human beings have selected as
interesting or extraordinary, and which nature
would discard if left to itself. For this reason they
look better planted near the house, not out in the
wider landscape. Purple foliage and yellow-leaved
forms also imply human habitation, as do the
extraordinary pink leaves of *Acer pseudoplatanus*
'Brilliantissimum'. In the wild, a purple tree such as
Fagus sylvatica 'Atropurpurea' would be simply a
blot on the landscape. The dreary canopy of *Prunus
cerasifera* 'Pissardii' is a disaster anywhere. Real
purists also feel that the blue-grey-green of some
eucalyptus makes them look as though they have
lost their way in those parts of the world where trees
are normally shades of green.

CONIFERS

Most conifers are strong characters. Their dark
colour and clear-cut outline makes them high-
impact plants, which means that many of them
make a major statement when planted as specimens.
Mixing conifers with other trees is not that easy.
A cluster of the same species always looks fine,
but most conifers come into the category of being
"family-only mixers", happy to be planted with
each other, but not blending easily with trees whose
shape and outline is very different. For example, one
could grow one large silver fir (*Abies*) on its own as
a specimen, or you could certainly plant a cluster of
silver firs of the same species. You might get away
with a cluster of different silver firs (same genus but
different species), given a little thought. You might
even group them with *Picea* species, which are related
and have a similar "Christmas tree" shape. But with
other trees which have a different but equally strong
character, any fir will look out at elbows. They could
be successfully planted with selected deciduous trees

BELOW Some strong-charactered trees mix happily only with other trees of the same species, or genus. Silhouetted against the blue sky of a summer's day, this cluster of cedars of Lebanon can be found at Upton House, Warwickshire.

as neighbours, since as we have seen, these blend easily. But a mixed bag of assorted conifers is commonly a disaster.

Plant an assortment of *Abies*, *Picea*, *Larix*, *Pinus*, *Chamaecyparis*, *Juniperus*, and *Thuja* together, and the effect will be like a family of eccentrics who don't speak to each other and meet only at funerals. With so many strong shapes juxtaposed, the result will be uncomfortable and and unnatural. What is lacking is the feeling of unity that natural habitats possess— somehow we feel instinctively that the way nature does it is right, and what we have instead looks like an assortment of vases on a shelf. One may see a

mixed pine and birch forest in some mountain regions, or one *Picea* and one *Larix* species living together (in the Glacier National Park in Montana, for instance), and the randomly repeated mixture of the same two species is pleasing. But if there is one of everything the result is hectic, because all those "ones" are strong, argumentative shapes.

A collection of conifers grouped together in a particular area of an arboretum almost always looks much less satisfying than its deciduous equivalent, and the reason is this reluctance to mix, and too many unrelated high-impact plants in close proximity. Conifers also lack the light and shade of deciduous

trees. Even in nature a coniferous forest is a lot darker and gloomier than a deciduous one. If the same dark green colour and the same branching habit continues without a break along the edge of a woodland walk, or where the trees open out into a clearing, the effect is liable to be monotonous. To break the conifers with clusters of deciduous trees always helps to bring some variety into the scheme—a break from that continuous dark green. One simple solution is to plant a drift of silver birch here and there, the white stems contrasting with the dark branches of

the conifers, but other species could easily be used, especially lightweight or feathery trees such as gleditsia or robinia. Many sorbus and the smaller acers are also useful species for mixing with conifers. A deciduous shrub layer can also help, or if the garden is on acid soil, some tastefully chosen, pale-coloured Ghent, Mollis, or Occidentalis azaleas.

LOLLIPOPS AND MONKEY PUZZLES

Some restraint, therefore, is definitely needed in the number of different conifer species that are planted in

immediate juxtaposition within the garden. Counted mong the "family-only mixers" are *Abies*, *Austrocedrus*, *Cedrus*, *Cryptomeria*, *Picea*, *Pseudotsuga*, *Sciadopitys*, *Sequoia*, *Sequoiadendron*, and *Tsuga*, along with *Chamaecyparis nootkatensis*, *C. obtusa*, and *C. pisifera*; *Cupressus arizonica*; and *Pinus nigra* subsp. *maritima*. Larch and tamarack (*Larix*) are not quite so dominant in the garden, partly because of their softer outline, and partly because they are deciduous trees, and the same applies to *Metasequoia* and *Taxodium*.

Pines (my favourites) are not as difficult to associate with other trees as are the pointed conifers, because of their irregular, seemingly windswept outlines. Nevertheless they too look best when treated as family-only mixers. As for monkey puzzle trees (*Araucaria*), they are renowned for their inability to blend with any other trees. "What should you plant with a monkey puzzle tree?" is the well-known question. The glade of monkey puzzles at Biddulph Grange in Shropshire provides the definitive answer: "Another monkey puzzle tree".

Yew (*Taxus baccata*) has a more bushy and less statuesque shape than the conifers listed above, and is therefore easier to position in the garden than the tall Christmas-tree shapes. Unclipped yew blends happily with deciduous plantings and is also fairly friendly towards other conifers. Other lower and bushy conifers that are also fairly accommodating in design terms and have a similar habit are *Athrotaxis*, *Cephalotaxus*, *Cupressus glabra*, *Fitzroya*, *Podocarpus*, *Saxegothaea*, and *Thujopsis dolabrata*.

One important and frequently planted category of conifers remains—the ones with a strong, neat, columnar shape—and most of these need very careful placing. *Chamaecyparis*, *Calocedrus*, *Cupressus*, *Juniperus*, and *Thuja*—these genera consist mainly of lollipop-shaped, or even pencil-point trees, and some restraint is called for in using them in the garden. They work well as accent plants—for example,one sometimes sees a matching pair either side of an opening, but this will inevitably look quite formal and designed. If you stick to using exactly the same species, there is usually less of a problem: dot them (that is, keep dotting the same species), cluster them, or plant them in rows in a formal context and they will look good, although dominant. It's when you plant one each of twenty-three different lollipop-shaped conifers that chaos reigns. This is a classic example where the principles that govern the appearance of the garden conflict with the agenda of our alter ego who has a Wants List in a back pocket.

OPPOSITE Achieving full potential. This example of *Phellodendron amurense*, the Amur Cork tree, from the Far East, has been grown as a specimen tree at the Royal Horticultural Society garden, Wisley, Surrey.

BELOW Some trees are picturesque and irregular in their outline and habit, such as the deciduous *Cercis siliquastrum*, the Judas tree. Hardy in temperate gardens although it comes from the Eastern Mediterranean region.

When an assortment of dwarf conifers is planted in various colour variations, the problem can be even worse. One green plus one yellow, one fat and one thin, one tall and one short: the result not infrequently seen is mayhem.

SPECIMEN TREES

Some trees ask to be planted together in naturalistic drifts; others are so remarkable that they deserve to be treated as specimen trees. It is difficult to define what qualifies a tree for this status, although there are some correspondences with leadership qualities. It is probably easier to explain what we are looking for by describing some examples. A typical *Sorbus* is small, slight, and frail, often looking a little lost—these are quite the wrong characteristics for a specimen tree. Set on its own beside a large lawn, a *Sorbus* simply fails to impress. The classic specimen tree, on the other hand, is the cedar of Lebanon (*Cedrus libani*). Magnificent, grand, stately, and strong are the adjectives commonly used to describe the effect of this tree, which demands to be given full scope to develop its potential. Compare it with a laburnum—if you dare. A laburnum has a wonderful display of flowers in late spring, and its ubiquity in suburban gardens should not blind us to its charms. But look at it out of flowering time—it leans awkwardly, as if it were lacking backbone. Its foliage and boughs look dirty and black, and the seed pods linger in ugly, drooping brown cases. No, the laburnum looks weak, and has too many faults to be considered as a specimen tree.

Specimen trees have "presence" of some kind—they have a picturesque outline, distinctive shape,

interesting foliage, or surprising flowers. In a field or a park-like situation an argument can well be made for the English oak (*Quercus robur*) as a specimen. Craggy and strong, it has wonderful presence in summer and winter, and somehow is the quintessential lion among trees. The London plane (*Platanus* × *hispanica*) is another admirable tree that deserves to be given full scope, with its twisting boughs reminiscent of human limbs, its open habit, the curious way it sheds its bark, and the pendulous globes of seed. It looks better in an open setting than on the side of the street: creating a tall trunk to allow a double-decker London bus to pass under it spoils its proportions. But this is a slightly more horticultural-looking tree than the oak, not really suitable for the countryside.

BELOW AND BELOW
RIGHT *Pinus pinea*, a
picturesque coniferous tree.
Trees of this species in the
Mediterranean region usually
have a longer main trunk
than this old example
growing at Kew Gardens.

Other notable picturesque trees include *Robinia pseudoacacia*, the false acacia; *Koelreuteria paniculata*, the so-called golden rain tree; *Cercis siliquastrum*, the Judas tree; several of the *Eucalyptus* species; *Morus nigra*, the black mulberry; *Salix babylonica* var. *pekinensis* 'Tortuosa'; *Sophora japonica*, the Pagoda tree; *Styrax japonicus*; and smaller subjects such as *Acer palmatum*. In varying degrees, these trees may exhibit asymmetry, irregular habit, gnarled boughs, or have graceful branches, and so on to recommend them.

The finest examples of distinctive shape and outline are the pines, whose praises I have sung previously. One or two are conical and symmetrical but most species are unpredictably and pleasingly picturesque in their appearance. The Scots pine, *Pinus sylvestris*, becomes increasingly irregular as it matures; on the other hand I regret that it's quite so blue in colour. There are too many wonderful pines—*P. ayacahuite*, *P. cembra*, *P. coulteri*, *P. densiflora*, *P. engelmannii*, *P. montezumae*, *P. nigra* subsp. *nigra*, *P. parviflora*, *P. pinea*, *P. ponderosa*, *P. radiata*, *P. thunbergii*, or *P. wallichiana*. I can't choose.

Some people select a tree for its bark. But unless it is very striking, as in the case of birches or some eucalyptus, it seems odd to me to select such an unimportant feature—a bit like saying you chose your husband because he had such nice legs. It makes much more sense to choose a tree for its autumn foliage, and there is a long list beyond *Acer palmatum*, the first that springs to mind. With some trees, the quality of their foliage impresses us all through the season, as with *Idesia polycarpa*. Some have very large leaves, such as ailanthus, catalpas, and *Pterocarya fraxinifolia*. Others have finely cut leaves, such as the cut-leaved beech, *Fagus sylvatica*

BELOW Laden with flowers held on largely bare stems early in spring—highly desirable, *Magnolia × soulangeana* growing in a Gloucestershire garden.

var. *heterophylla* 'Aspleniifolia'. Be warned, however, that trees chosen for the size of their leaves can make an awful mess in the autumn. The fallen leaves of *Catalpa* and the fig tree, *Ficus carica*, for instance, are not a pretty sight.

When it comes to flowers, the most remarkable trees are the magnolias. I don't count rhododendrons, which are really giant shrubs. There is simply nothing to beat *Magnolia × soulangeana* and its cultivars for the shape and colour of their flowers. The smaller magnolias are particularly useful, since their flowers are conveniently arranged at eye level where they can be admired by passers-by. Paulownias have unusual flowers, but they are up in the sky somewhere, and you'd need to build a tower to appreciate them.

7
Trees, gardens, and arboreta

Compared with other types of gardening, growing trees is not particularly labour-intensive, and on the whole trees give a great deal of pleasure. The first task will be to consider whether the soil or microclimate will impose any limitations on the kinds of trees that can be grown. Whether the soil is acid or alkaline will have a major impact on the choices one can make. Sea spray and high winds are further unchangeable facts of life. Poor drainage and the existence of damp areas of ground may also have to be taken into account: one can put in land drains, at some expense, or alternatively consider the merits of alders, willows, and other trees that enjoy damp conditions. It only makes sense to grow plants that will do well on the site that we have. One can cosset one or two small treasures, but persuading a large number of unhappy trees to grow is a waste of money and effort.

GROUNDS FOR OPTIMISM
Several acres are needed for a scheme that can boast the label "tree collection". In gardens of between a quarter of an acre and three acres, quite a number of trees can be grown, especially if small ones are chosen. But if they are large-scale forest trees, the size of beech or oaks, they will turn out to be very dominant, easily dwarfing the rest of the garden. Lawns and planted areas near such trees need to be large enough and bold enough in scale to match the height and scale of the trees. Trees also create shade, and this will affect the kind of gardening that will succeed underneath them or nearby.

One can plant a trees-only arboretum, but if the trees are to be mixed with a range of shrubs, bulbs,

OPPOSITE Birches can be
planted for their own sake,
but they are also useful as
temporary "fillers" while
other, more exotic and
expensive trees are growing
to their full size. This is
Betula utilis var. *jacquemontii*
growing at Cambridge
University Botanic Garden.

BELOW Too close for
comfortable tree-viewing:
Abies nordmanniana
crowded in with other trees.
Allowing for the future size
of a large tree is an
important but difficult
discipline when creating a
tree collection.

and perennials it is worth remembering that the range of plants that will tolerate a permanent degree of shade is limited. Although many of the so-called "woodlanders" are very attractive, they are often small and reticent, and don't possess the colour and flamboyance of sun-loving perennials. Most people will not want the whole of their garden to be shady: woodland gardens are really for those with a pre-established wood and plenty of space. Trees take a lot of moisture and nutrients out of the ground, with their extensive root run. However, this does vary, depending on the species and how close to the surface their roots grow. Beech and birch are notoriously shallow-rooted, and beech woods are well known for being relatively bare at ground level, especially those established on thin soils.

GARDEN, HOUSE, AND LANDSCAPE

To plant trees because they interest you is one thing, but it's worth remembering that trees can also be planted for practical reasons—to provide protection from wind, for instance, to give privacy, or to screen out an unwanted view. Once the horticultural limitations of a site have been addressed, these functional, less decorative plantings should be considered next, before the purely ornamental trees go in.

To plant a tree is not necessarily a Good Thing, although this is often assumed. Trees can easily destroy views that were worth retaining. As many historic landscapes have been spoilt by an excess of trees as have been destroyed by tree-felling. Sometimes these view-blocking trees were planted in well-meaning error, but sometimes they were simply self-sown. One very common area where this hap-

pens is beside a lake or a pond. Undergrowth easily develops at the water's edge; this in turn allows ash seedlings or young sycamores to take root, and before anyone has noticed, a long view down to the water has been lost. Before planting that delicate little sapling it is well worth standing back and estimating its effect in ten years' time. If the house has a

Views are almost always an asset to be preserved, whether into the far distance or simply over the nearby landscape. If we "discover" a view as we go round a tree collection it provides a change of focus for the eye. Trees have a framing effect, and a view is usually enhanced when seen between trees, or through an opening in a plantation, since the frame of branches somehow flatters the view. The frame may be in the immediate foreground, or it may be a break in a more distant tree belt. In some cases there may be the additional pleasure of coming across the view suddenly. This is the so-called "surprise" effect, more properly called "sequential contrast". Trees can also be planted to create perspective. This involves planting a tree or a scattering of trees in the middle distance, in positions which will improve or enhance a more distant view.

In a countryside setting, thought may need to be given to the relationship of the trees we want to plant to those that grow in the adjoining landscape. What will the collection look like from the outside? There will be many trees that will blend in perfectly with the established landscape, but others may not. The main thing to grasp here is the distinction between a "horticultural" tree and a native one. Certain plants, while beautiful in themselves, look alien seen against countryside where nothing native resembles them. Atlantic cedars, for example, are attractive as trees, but their grey-blue colour means that they are out of place in a temperate landscape where all the trees are green. An Australian setting, among the silvery grey of eucalyptus, might suit them very well, but in a northerly European or American landscape, horticultural trees such as blue

pleasant view to the distant hills, will this new tree eventually make that view invisible?

If we move into a new garden it is worth checking whether we could open up a worthwhile prospect by taking out one or two trees. There is no reason why a tree collection has to be wholly inward-looking.

LEFT If there had been a little less planting under this multi-stem eucalyptus, the pale-coloured trunks would have shown up to better advantage.

BELOW A dwarf conifer loses out in the battle with a big pine tree.

cedars or other exotic conifers are best planted in the immediate vicinity of the house, where artificiality can reasonably be expected.

Farther away from the house one should try to assess whether the plants we propose will make any impact on the general environment and, if necessary, exercise a degree of restraint. For example, it's worth bearing in mind that many large conifers will grow considerably taller than the average deciduous tree. Wellingtonias (*Sequoiadendron giganteum*), *Pseudotsuga menziesii* (the Douglas fir), and several of the larger *Picea* and *Abies* species fall into this category. Their pointed tops will eventually stick up above the undulating canopy of a piece of native woodland; this may be of no consequence, but on the skyline it can look obtrusive. On the other hand, where the native landscape is essentially deciduous woodland, many deciduous trees from other parts of the world can be treated as "pseudo-natives". From a distance, you can forget those interesting nuances of leaf shape and so on. Most exotic species of oak, ash, or lime will easily pass themselves off as natives in any landscape where English oak and beech are the native woodland tree, as will *Nothofagus*, *Carya*, or *Pterocarya*.

The relationship of trees to the house also deserves careful thought. On clay soils, trees with hungry roots such as poplars and willows need to be kept away from the foundations. Nevertheless, as we walk round our tree collection we shall want to be able to look back at the house, and see it in an attractive setting. It is usually thought desirable to

frame the view of the house from certain viewpoints, for instance from the entrance gates. One of the attractions of Batsford Arboretum, in Gloucestershire, is that as the visitor walks along looking at the trees, the paths circle round the very large house, creating glimpses of it from various angles. Views of the hills and the wider landscape outside the arboretum create further interest, providing a break from endless trees and greenery. This is a feature which several more famous arboreta lack.

SPACE, TIME, AND ARBORETA

If you are considering planting trees, a major consideration in laying out a tree collection is the question of the correct spacing. How far apart should the trees be? There is a balancing act to be carried out here. Every tree needs its own space to grow in, since it will be very annoying later on to discover that two equally rare and quite different trees have been planted too close together (although I see this in almost every arboretum I know). This problem is

particularly troublesome if the habit and shape of the trees in question contrast strongly. If nothing is done, they will look more uncomfortable every year, and both will become misshapen. If one inherits this problem, a decision should be made as soon as possible about which tree should be taken out. If both trees are equally desirable, and either would look good in the space they currently occupy, the answer is usually that the weaker of the two should go—if there is a weaker one. The sooner this is dealt with the better, before they start to lean sideways or adopt an ungainly outline.

Another awkward feature often seen is a cluster of shrubs that have grown larger than anticipated and are jostling a tree, preventing us seeing its shape to advantage. Any tree whose bark or trunk is interesting or whose habit and shape is good needs to be underplanted with a very low shrub layer: otherwise there will be a collision as the shrub pushes up under the branches of the tree.

But if every individual tree in the collection is a fully grown, isolated specimen, this can also look odd. For a start, it is unnatural for groups of trees to have so much space, as if each tree had a contagious disease and would contaminate the next if it touched it. If they all hardly meet at the fingertips, they will all be perfect specimens, but anyone who wants to see the tree in question will still want to stand back somewhere without having to step into the shadow of the next tree.

The most sensible approach is to decide that some trees will be clustered or grouped, while others are to be specimens. This was the strategy adopted by Capability Brown in the eighteenth century. He

BELOW Some trees are attractive in themselves but don't sit happily in their landscape context: blue *Cedrus atlantica* looking incongruous in an English landscape park.

BELOW Glimpses of the house at Batsford Arboretum, in Gloucestershire, help to orientate the visitor and make a contrast to continual greenery.

planted large numbers of trees in perimeter belts or in rounded clumps, but around the edges of these mass plantings he placed detached specimen trees, looking as if they had broken away from the rest, to soften the outline of the mass plantings. It is much more natural for trees to be in drifts and create a quasi-woodland habitat, especially with groups of the same species or closely related species. This means that anyone who wants to collect trees of one particular genus (*Sorbus*, *Betula*, or *Fraxinus*, for instance) can plant them reasonably close together so that there is some blending when they are seen from a distance. Because trees of the same genus tend to have similar growth patterns, most will look happy together. The strong-charactered trees can then be planted on their own, as specimens, floating free from these belts or drifts.

However, being in the same genus, or being a variety of a certain species, doesn't guarantee that the habit will be the same. One variety may, for example, have

a stiffly upright habit, while all the others are grace-fully broad-spreading. Similarly *Betula medwedewii* has a wide-spreading habit that is quite different from the average birch. In such cases the atypical tree cannot be expected to merge with the others in the grouping.

The issue that cannot be avoided is time. Trees take time to grow. Planting semi-mature trees gives an immediate effect, but they may take surprisingly

BELOW Occasional long-distance views are always worth retaining—as here at Batsford Arboretum, where the shadowy line of distant hills beyond the house forms an added dimension to the garden.

long to establish and will certainly be very expensive. In a matter of a few years a younger tree will catch up with the larger one. Young trees, on the other hand, hardly take up any space, but the effect in the short term may be sparse and disappointing. One solution is to plant several trees of one species together and fell the additional ones later. This works with the more common, inexpensive trees, but does create a lot of extra work a few years later.

More likely, the temptation will be to forget the plan, and let the extra trees remain even when they have outlived their original purpose.

Another solution is to plant "fillers". In other words, among the carefully chosen and unusual trees one can scatter groups of more common ones such as birch. This will create a more instant woodland effect, but similar problems arise. Again it will be easy to forget that the birch trees were supposed to be cut down after five years' time, and it will seem a waste of effort to have grown them only to cut them down again. In a case like this, the young gardener should be patient, but the old may be forgiven if they are not.

Trees come in various sizes, according to standard nursery practice, with names such as seedlings, transplants, standards, and semi-mature trees all indicating a given range of sizes. Which to choose depends entirely on the situation. Semi-mature trees tend to be so expensive that they are beyond the purse of most private individuals, while seedlings are extremely cheap and may be bought by the hundred, or even thousand. A good size tree to choose is one with a girth of approximately four inches (between 8 and 10 cm), and a height of between eight and a half and ten feet (2.75 and 3 m)—it's big enough to make a bit of impact, but not so large that it will take a long time to establish itself.

A tree collection always remains an on-going project. It's never static. It may be labour-saving, but every spring and autumn there will still be jobs to be done, which may well be more elaborate than with other kinds of gardening, and may occasionally require the professional help of a tree surgeon, or

BELOW It's difficult to understand why this new sapling has been planted so close to a magnificent, mature specimen of *Abies grandis*.

arboriculturist. This will be the time to assess the growth and spread of the trees, to take out a poor specimen here, replace a failure there, and decide if anything needs to be added.

STAKES AND MISTAKES

When it comes to planting the trees which are to be "enjoyed"—in other words, trees that have been chosen with care for their individual interest—we need to identify where the trees are to be seen from, and how best they are to be appreciated. How will they look from the windows of the house, for example, or some other key vantage point in the garden? If the site is at present a bare field, one should avoid imagining it as a blank canvas on which trees can be dotted at random, as if grown from seeds dropped by passing birds. As a practical aid it is always worth putting in large stakes where proposed trees are to go, and living with them for a while. Look at them from various angles. Walk to and fro. Try to imagine a mature tree at the point where the stake is. Some people find this is not an easy skill to acquire—one friend told me that she tries to imagine what it would be like if an elephant walked along at that moment and stood where the stake was. Of course, many trees are a lot larger than a passing elephant, but this was just an aid to her imagination. In addition there is the winter and the summer effect to consider, and in the case of acers, tupelos (*Nyssa*), amelanchiers, liquidambars and so on, the effect of autumn colour.

But before we put our stakes in the ground we first ought to consider the issue of geometry—or lack of it. As a single object in the landscape, a tree

Geometry breeds
formal avenues, and is best
on flat ground. An autumnal
view of liriodendrons and
cedars at Westonbirt
Arboretum, Gloucestershire.

may be considered as one dot, or one blob. However, when we place that "dot" on the ground, there is a variety of ways of relating it to its fellow dots, or connecting it in some way with other significant features in the landscape. For instance, we could mark out a straight line and carefully measure off where the trees are to go at regular intervals, in which case we shall produce a row. In countries where formal gardens are the predominant way of gardening, this will seem the normal thing to do. In England, where the English Landscape style is deep

in the national psyche, this would seem an alien thing to do. Instead the trees will be placed out of line, and the spaces between them will be varied, resulting simply in an informal group, drift, or cluster. A large, informal, more or less rounded group of trees we call a clump.

If a long line of trees are planted in pairs they will form an avenue, and this can be either straight or curving. A long band of trees, several trees wide, we call a belt. The areas of parkland around most great eighteenth-century English houses had perimeter belts that kept the "artistic" landscape in and the world of agriculture or industry out.

How we group our trees will depend on our temperament and on the overall style of the garden or the collection. Some people are allergic to straight lines, others complain at endlessly winding paths. Until the 1730s, in England, geometry was universally assumed to be the right way to plant. Since then a more relaxed partnership with nature has seemed more desirable. A stance has to taken on this issue when laying out large-scale gardens: do we impose some geometry or should there be irregular curves that follow the contours of the land? Formality works best on a level site—it usually looks uncomfortable on an irregular slope. It also suggests formal avenues and the repetition of the same tree, equally spaced in rows. If we want a collection of different, but possibly related trees, a more informal layout will probably be better.

THE PATH TO SUCCESS

The key to laying out a successful tree collection is something which has nothing to do with the trees themselves, nor with which tree goes with which, but it applies to every collection. The arrangement of paths through the trees is perhaps the most important issue of all. Trees are best seen from a path, not by zig-zagging at random across a grassy field: it seems necessary to point this out. To appreciate the trees as carefully chosen and nurtured individuals, the ideal situation is for the owner (and the visitor) to be able to walk around the collection by means of a clear, convenient route, and for the best trees to be displayed to advantage along the way. This may

sound obvious, but is rarely done. This tree-viewing route would then lead back to base, avoiding any awkward or misleading dead ends, and would also avoid a return journey over the same ground. In other words, a simple circular route is the ideal, though the word "circular" is obviously not to be understood in its strict sense: in fact the path may have to twist quite a few times or curl about as it goes on its way.

If the tree collection is to be open to visitors, it is particularly useful if this path takes in as much of the site as possible. Nothing interesting should be missed, and there should be no chance of getting lost or feeling confused about which way to go. Ideally one ought to be able to inspect the whole collection from a path which is either level, or has an easy gradient. A mown grass path, wide enough for two people to walk together, is the ideal minimum. To have to wander into long grass is not at all convenient, although of course it may be necessary to step aside now and again to study the detail of a flower or some berries.

A distinction can be made here between the owner's experience of a large garden, and the visitor's experience. Obviously the owner is not going to get lost in his own garden, but for the garden visitor it is very useful to have a clear idea of the route one should take. Curators of large-scale gardens and arboreta open to the public are naturally familiar with their own gardens, but when the visitor tries to find the way round, it is often very confusing. Many large arboreta have grown up over the course of several decades and have been added to bit by bit, and their layout has become so complex, wayward, and

seemingly irrational that a map is essential for the visitor. Only after one's third or fourth visit can one have any confidence about choosing a route through the grounds, or even finding one's way out, and this seems regrettable.

If the shape of the site is complex, a hierarchy of paths can be established. In other words, in addition to the main circular route there can be occasional small diversions or loops off the main path, which before long lead safely back to the main route. These detours can be distinguished by being narrower, or having a different surface from the main path. Sadly, in many large gardens and arboreta it seems to be no good expecting the width of a path or its type of surface to give us any indication of its priority or usefulness in leading us through the grounds. How often one follows a large gravel path, only to find it stops dead without warning and one is presented with a choice of smaller grassy tracks, with no indication where each leads. Right? Left? A quick study of the map is needed before we get totally lost.

An irregular or informal grid layout is a common feature of large arboreta, often degenerating into little mazy paths that proliferate among smaller-scale shrub plantings. Although a network of paths gives multiple choices to the visitor, enabling us to wander at will, it also makes it virtually impossible to traverse every path or avenue (and therefore see every interesting tree) in one visit, without a great deal of double-tracking. Do we go methodically up and down the north-south paths, and ignore all the east-west ones? A grid-iron pattern may (or may not) be a rational way to plan cities, but it is hardly an inspired choice for a garden. However, if the paths twist and bend too much we may lose our sense of direction altogether. Is it safe to wander idly according to what takes our fancy? Whichever way we go, something worthwhile will be missed. If all we want is a pleasant setting for walk while we chat among ourselves, it doesn't matter, but if, like me, you are a serious tree-spotter, it can be frustrating.

BELOW A bridge at Abbotsbury Subtropical Gardens, Dorset. After meandering among the trees, the brilliant colour of the bridge and the darkness of the water make you feel you have arrived at some kind of memorable goal.

A SENSE OF ARRIVAL

In addition to routes, a garden also needs destinations. The author Robert Louis Stevenson may have said that it is better to travel hopefully than to arrive, but that is a poor way to lay out a garden.

Too many gardens consist of meandering paths that seem to travel nowhere—not even back to the entrance. It is much more satisfying to feel that at some point we have arrived, that we have reached what we came to see, even if half the pleasure was in what we saw along the way. So if or when we actually find the pagoda at Kew Gardens, we feel we have

got somewhere—we haven't just spent the day wandering along gravel paths and grassy walks. Similarly, at the so-called subtropical gardens at Abbotsbury, in the south of England, after wandering here and there it is a relief to discover dark, secretive and lushly planted pools, crossed by attractive bridges painted a dazzling Chinese red.

A more radical example is that paragon of English gardens, Stourhead in Wiltshire, which is both an eighteenth-century landscape garden as well as a nineteenth-century plant collection. One sees excellent trees along the path round the lake, and also

attractive, scented flowers at rhododendron time, in a collection dating from the early nineteenth century. But the journey is paced and landmarked by a succession of features and spaces which make us feel that the journey had a destination as well as a road: first the Temple of Flora, then the grotto, the Pantheon, and the temple of Apollo. We didn't just drift aimlessly among the trees: we went somewhere memorable and we came back. "The garden, like every other work of art, should have a climax" says Sir George Sitwell, in his book *On the Making of Gardens*, and later he declares "To make a great gar-

den you must have a great idea; a cypress causeway leading to a giant's castle or a fountain cave …" Over the top, I know, as Sitwell's prose often is, but you get the idea.

It's not my intention to suggest that every tree collection has to include some expensive built feature or remarkable gimmick. All I recommend is that the paths open out every now and again into a grassy space, and that this is made memorable in some way by its shape, its plants, or its view, a place where we can sit down for a few moments to relax, enjoy, and admire.

8
Climbers and wall shrubs

ALL GARDENS HAVE BOUNDARIES, and when they are formed by walls and fences rather than hedges, they provide ready-made places for climbers. If the garden is bounded by hedges, then the walls of the house itself should not be forgotten, but a degree of common sense must be used here to avoid rampant climbers that might creep under eaves or obscure the windows. Taking a climber down from a wall once it has become established is a surprisingly tedious and time-consuming affair, as I found to my cost when I realized that the ivy on our house was getting out of control. There are several attractive climbers that one may well come to regret planting against the house—for example, the more vigorous kinds of *Vitis*, *Ampelopsis*, and *Parthenocissus*.

Many climbing plants are extremely beautiful in themselves and most gardeners will want to grow them for their own sake—climbing roses, for example, and clematis—but climbers also perform a very practical function in terms of design of the garden. One of their great advantages is that they soften the boundaries of a plot with greenery without taking up too much space, and for this reason alone climbing plants make an invaluable contribution to the average-sized town or suburban garden. Old and unattractive sheds and garages can be masked and camouflaged, and dreary walls and fences covered by leaves and flowers. But it's worth bearing in mind that if the boundaries are to be effectively hidden, at least half of the plants used for the purpose need to be evergreen so that the screening is effective during the winter season. This can present some difficulty, as the range of evergreen climbing plants is somewhat limited.

Shrubs can also be used to cover walls and fences, but how the term "wall shrub" ought to be defined is arguable. Usually it is taken to describe a slightly tender shrub that will survive more happily given the protection of a warm or sheltered wall. However, another way of defining a wall shrub is to think of it as a shrub that doesn't mind being trained and

winter clipping regime so that the flowering and berrying branches aren't lost due to pruning. Some gardeners claim that pyracanthas are unexciting, to which I reply that they have flowers (if unexceptional), brightly coloured berries in abundance, and evergreen leaves—what more do you want? Of course, one pyracantha is much like another and so they aren't collector's plants, but all the same they do have a useful purpose.

HOUSING A COLLECTION

For anyone who wants to make a collection of climbers, the difficulty is likely to be the lack of vertical surfaces to support them all. In the case of a tree collection, lack of space can sometimes be resolved by buying more land, but the solution to finding enough places for climbers is not so easy. Many genera of climbing plants, such as *Rosa* and *Clematis*, have a very large number of species and varieties, and the

clipped back drastically every so often, to prevent it from growing out too far from the wall and taking up too much space in the garden. Flowering quinces (*Chaenomeles*) work well, because they flower early and can be pruned after flowering, and although they have fruits, these aren't all that exciting. Pyracanthas are another example, but these need a late

BELOW For those wishing
to make a collection of
climbing plants, trellis may
be the best way to provide
all the vertical surfaces
necessary to provide the
required support. This
slightly "artistic" trellis is
in a garden designed by
the author.

amount of vertical surface needed for even a modest collection of these plants is liable to be excessive.

Large gardens that have been divided up into separate spaces, or "garden rooms", have a distinct advantage over their smaller or more informal counterparts, as the walls of their "compartments" can provide ready-made places for climbers to be established. But if the divisions are made with hedges of yew, box, or beech, the effect will be wonderfully solid but yield no opportunity for growing climbers. One does occasionally see the scarlet *Tropaeolum speciosum* scrambling over a yew hedge, but this isn't as artless an effect as it looks. To train a climbing plant on to, over, or through a hedge that has to be clipped is a tricky business, only to be attempted by the patient and long-suffering.

Walls provide the ideal support for many climbers. Some species will cling to a wall unaided;

others need wires. Some need vertical wires as well as horizontal ones. It all depends what the chosen plant prefers, and this will require some forethought and planning on the part of the garden owner. But high garden walls are not cheap to build, and may be an impractical option for many garden owners. In this case it may be a good idea to reserve the walls of the house for a few climbers that need the most support—wisteria being a classic example, often high on the Wants List of many plant lovers. Lighter, less expensive materials can then be used to create screens and divisions within the garden. Trellis is most likely to be the chosen option when cost is an issue, and while some plants need the solidity of a wall, others actually prefer an open trellis through which the wind can blow.

Before long stretches of trellis are introduced into the garden, careful consideration has to be given to the impact this will have on the garden as a whole. To introduce walls or lengths of trellis into the garden is to structure and compartmentalize it in a major way, and because trellis is usually set at a height above eye level, it functions visually as a wall, albeit a slightly gappy one. Walls and trellises will block existing views (except where there are openings), and care has to be taken that what is seen through any opening is worthy of the focus of attention it will now receive. A new trellis screen should not be thought of as an exhibition stand or display board that can be placed on a whim anywhere within an existing room. It also has to be borne in mind that for every additional "sunny side" that the new screen creates, there will be an opposing, shadier one, and this will influence the plants that can be

grown. We need to take care to site any new vertical surfaces in such a way that the spaces that result from the division have their own logic, are of reasonable size, and are a good, coherent shape, such as a simple square or rectangle—not some awkward, left-over-looking triangular plot.

Because it is natural for walls, fences, and trellises to adopt a straight line, areas specially created for climbers will look best when quite formal in design. A geometrical curve such as a semi-circle can work as long it does not form too tight an arc. Making a trellis follow a wiggly line is not a good idea, because it defies the logic of the materials used, and the resulting spaces created are also likely to be odd.

EVERGREEN WALL SHRUBS

For the gardener who wants to provide a soft and leafy edge to the garden all the year around, rather than house a large collection, there are many good evergreen shrubs that can be used. But unfortunately, many of these evergreens are so vigorous that they require frequent clipping back, and this doesn't always work. I've tried both *Elaeagnus* × *ebbingei* and *E. macrophylla* against a wall and ended up in a constant battle trying to keep them in order. The variegated *Elaeagnus* cultivars might tolerate it, as they are slightly less vigorous. Choisya is another shrub that looks unassuming, but actually demands a lot of garden space as it gets older. If you hack at it too often it either looks too obviously clipped, or else ends up in an unsightly mess. I've also tried *Bupleurum fruticosum* against a wall, but this spends its whole life trying to arch forwards into a big mound, so I can't recommend it as a wall shrub. *Viburnum tinus* and *Prunus lusitanica*, together with their variegated forms, also prefer to be left in peace to grow outwards and upwards. Hollies should definitely be banned from the back of any border. If you want to clip them back they are awkward to handle, and their fallen leaves are a real pain when you are pulling up weeds.

Many good evergreen wall shrubs are too borderline for growing in temperate gardens and need a Zone 9 climate, as found only in the mildest parts of the British Isles, or in the southern states of the USA. In this category are many *Abutilon* species, along with several acacias, *Acradenia frankliniae*, most azaras, callistemons, *Carpenteria californica*, some ceanothus, cestrums, clianthus, *Acca sellowiana* (formerly *Feijoa selloana*), fremontodendron, *Itea*, piptanthus and vestias. Having said this, the British climate has been getting milder over recent years and at the moment both a callistemon and *Itea ilicifolia* are growing happily against a wall in my sheltered Gloucestershire garden.

In practice any evergreen shrub that can be described as slow-growing can be used as a wall shrub, in the clippable sense of the word. To discover whether the shrub you admire is slow-growing is not always that easy, but in this category are several *Cotoneaster* species and varieties, and with their generous displays of berries in the autumn, these are not to be despised. Other possibilities are *Osmanthus delavayi*, some kinds of euonymus, and the escallonias 'Iveyi', 'Edinensis', and 'Langleyensis'.

Box (*Buxus*) doesn't have to be free-standing, but can equally well be planted in front of a fence. In fact I have spent many years successfully persuading a slow-growing, slightly variegated box to screen a six feet (1.8 m) length of fence without coming out into the border more than six inches (15 cm). *Magnolia grandiflora* is a wonderful wall shrub, but a "classy" plant like this demands a good architectural wall, and the walls of the house are best. *Ribes speciosum* should also be used to ornament a good wall, rather than screen it.

Slow-growing evergreen shrubs will be no use if we want an unattractive wall or fence to be obscured as soon as possible. A better solution here would be to plant bamboos. Graceful, evergreen, and with plenty of height, they will soon screen any undesirable fence or wall. The snag is, of course, that many of them spread and grow too large. It is not that they spread so fast, but the relentlessness of their forward march that causes the problem. Root control put in when they are planted is the answer, in the form of a thick, impenetrable plastic barrier material manufactured for the purpose, and it does not have to go down all that deep, since many bamboo roots keep fairly close to the surface.

CHOOSING EVERGREEN CLIMBERS

When it comes to climbing plants, as opposed to wall shrubs, limitations of hardiness apply to a whole range of evergreens—if we are still looking for year-round cover. In this category come *Asteranthera ovata*, *Billardiera longiflora*, *Dregea sinensis*, *Gelsemium sempervirens*, *Holboellia latifolia*, *Jasminum fruticans* and *J. × stephanense*, *Kadsura japonica*, *Lapageria rosea*, *Lardizabala biternata*, *Mutisia*, *Semele androgyna*, *Senecio scandens*, *Solanum jasminoides*, and *Stauntonia hexaphylla*, which are all Zone 8 or 9 plants—on the borderline of hardiness in most temperate zones—and require milder areas and a sheltered spot (or indeed the warmth of a conservatory). Hardier than most of the above is the coral plant, *Berberidopsis corallina*, which is a good plant, although rarely seen, and requiring little support. Nevertheless it, too, is unlikely to succeed in colder regions.

This leaves surprisingly few evergreen climbers that can be reliably grown in frost-prone gardens: *Hedera*, a few untypical evergreen *Clematis* species, one climbing *Hydrangea*, and a few species of *Lonicera*, *Pileostegia*, and *Trachelospermum*. Of these, *Hedera* (ivy) is the most common, although not everyone admires it. It does need keeping in check, but this is not a very difficult task, and personally I think it an extremely useful plant. There is a huge range of cultivars, and although few people

BELOW Unfortunately, the range of good evergreen climbers hardy in temperate gardens is rather small. This is *Solanum crispum*, a vigorous, evergreen climber in the potato family.

would have the necessary space or inclination to house a specialized collection, there are among them many stylish and variegated forms. The important thing to look out for when buying an unfamiliar ivy is to make sure it is actually a climbing one. Some are merely "trailers", suitable for ground cover, hanging baskets, or for growing as indoor plants, and lack the vigour that is required to climb a wall. Although

some ivies have impressively large leaves, such as *Hedera colchica* 'Dentata Variegata' and 'Sulphur Heart', in many ways the smaller-leaved forms look neater, and are less likely to be damaged by cold or windy weather.

The evergreen clematis most commonly seen is C. *armandii*, which has a slightly exotic air to it, flowering earlier than other clematis. With its large,

glossy leaflets in threes, this is an attractive species for a warm, sheltered spot; in exposed positions it can look ragged and bedraggled as a result of cold or wind damage. The so-called Virgin's bower, *Clematis cirrhosa*, is a winter-flowering evergreen, but completely different from *C. armandii*, and more like a less vigorous relative of *C. montana*. The variety *balearica* is hardier, and usually preferable, while the cultivar 'Freckles' is said to be an improvement on both. All three prefer a sunny aspect, but suffer less in cold weather than *C. armandii*. There are other evergreen clematis species, such as *C. brachiata* and *C. hookeriana*, but these are rarely listed and may be challenging to track down.

The best-known evergreen honeysuckle is *Lonicera japonica*, which has an attractive scent and a long

flowering season, but is also a rampant grower and untidy, which makes it hard to recommend. *L. henryi* is also very vigorous and its flowers are rather small compared with its cousins. *L. splendida* is a species that deserves to be seen more often: a fast-growing, evergreen relation of the British native *L. periclymenum*, it needs a sunny, sheltered wall to thrive. Several other good honeysuckles will retain their leaves during mild winters, and are variously called semi-evergreen or semi-deciduous: *L. etrusca*, *L. sempervirens*, and *L. × brownii*.

Among other evergreen climbers, *Trachelospermum jasminoides* is an attractive, twining plant with fragrant flowers that performs best on a warm and sun-facing wall. *Trachelospermum asiaticum* is hardier, but its flowers are smaller. *Pileostegia* is a dark evergreen climber with leathery leaves, in the Hydrangeaceae: this is a good plant, which would be the answer to a prayer if only it was not so painfully slow to develop.

The climbing solanums are faster-growing: *S. crispum* is a large plant, good in itself and also useful for covering unsightly structures. It's a member of the potato family, as can be seen in its attractive clusters of flowers, with a purplish-blue corolla surrounding a cone of bright yellow anthers.

CHOOSING DECIDUOUS CLIMBERS

If it is flowers we primarily want, rather than year-round screening, we may choose from a vast selection of deciduous climbers. But while I wouldn't deny the charms of foliage plants such as *Vitis henryana*, or *Vitis coignetiae*, the attractions of three well-known genera greatly outweigh all others.

Rosa, *Clematis*, and *Lonicera* provide some of the most wonderful flowering plants that gardens can contain, more than enough for the most eclectic plant lover. To collect a wide range of these plants will clearly enhance any garden.

Of these three, the honeysuckles mostly look after themselves, but many climbing roses and most clematis cannot be treated merely as vertical surface-cover: they require care, attention, and skill, at the correct times during the year, if they are to look their best. Of the clematis, *C. montana* and its relatives are perhaps the easiest to care for, although they eventually build themselves into a huge tangle, that then has to be hacked at like the Gordian knot, and brought back to some form of order. Next in the rating of ease-of-care come the Viticella and Jackmannii types, of which there is an excellent selection, many available in rich, dark colours.

Among roses, the easiest are the ramblers. Many can safely be left to look after themselves, and simply snipped at occasionally. Personally I confess to lacking the dedication needed to look after those fussier climbing roses that have to have careful, selective pruning on an annual basis. Keen rosarians can write me off if they wish, but encouraging new vigorous growth by extracting the older branches, unthreading long arching stems heavily armed with vicious thorns—this is not a hobby I enjoy. So personally I opt for an easy life and choose easy-care roses—such as, 'Debutante', 'Excelsa', 'Goldfinch', 'Paul's Scarlet Climber', 'Phyllis Bide', 'Sander's White Rambler', 'Veilchenblau', and 'Wedding Day'—and apart from a trim here and there I leave them to get on with it.

9
Shrubs

"THE ANSWER IS SHRUBS", said the bold chapter heading in one of the first gardening books I ever read, and at first glance it does seem that shrubs have a lot to offer. However, after many years as a gardener I am not at all convinced they are the all-purpose, work-free, and colour-full answer to all gardening problems that is sometimes claimed. It's true that shrubs need comparatively little attention, especially when they are first planted. But the reality is that many of them just go on getting bigger and bigger, and this can end up being a nuisance where space is limited. Maybe I wanted a large shrub, but on the other hand, maybe I didn't—it's easy to buy and plant first, without realizing that your neat-looking, container-grown shrub is a cuckoo in the nest that eventually wants to be eight feet tall and ten feet across (2.5 m and 3 m). Or maybe double that, in the case of *Rosa xanthina* var. *hugonis*—judging from the one at Kew.

SIZE, GROWTH, AND VALUE

Size is the main issue that I have with shrubs: many of them are simply too large for the average garden. Their relentless growth means that when they are planted with other kinds of plants they turn out to be remarkably antisocial. They surreptitiously squeeze out neighbouring perennials and bulbs, until they die quietly due to lack of light or starvation beneath the shrub's ever-extending branches. Usually this is not the shrub's fault, but the gardener's, who planted the perennials too close to the shrub in the first place.

A related problem is that many shrubs are not particularly floriferous for their size, and may also

have a relatively short flowering season. Shrubby honeysuckles, for instance, come into this category—or, think of any of those winter- or early spring-flowering viburnums. In one of the coldest months of the year, when nobody is out in the garden, you get a spattering of deliciously scented but very small flowers. And the rest of the year you get leaves: a

BELOW *Rosa xanthina* f. *hugonis*. Size is the problem with many shrubs. This specimen, growing at Kew Gardens, is several yards across—far too large for the average garden.

BELOW *Syringa vulgaris* 'Lucie Baltet' at Kew Gardens. One or two lilacs is all most gardens could contain—to house a serious collection, a large institutional garden would be needed.

rounded mass of undistinguished foliage approximately eight feet high and six feet across (2.4 m and 1.8 m). In a large garden or public park this may be fine, but for my money a shrub like this doesn't pull its weight in the garden.

Shrub gardens, therefore, are either large gardens, or they are labour-saving and not-very-exciting gardens. However, shrubs are only labour-saving if they are planted at the right spacings in the first place, and sadly it isn't very easy to discover how big your plant is going to grow. Even the best books tend to be coy on the subject. It all depends, is what they will tell you. This is true, but unhelpful. Hillier's Manual[2] describes shrubs as large, medium, small, dwarf, or prostrate, which is better than nothing. But if the eventual size of a shrub is said to be somewhere between five and ten feet (1.5 and 3 m) high and the same across, this actually means that in terms of mass the largest possible specimen can be 800 per cent larger than the smallest.

THE SHRUB COLLECTION

There are relatively few shrubby genera that would inspire enough enthusiasm to lure the plant lover into collecting them. Shrub collections are fine for

rest of the year there will necessarily be a large blank area where nothing in particular is happening.

This is partly a question of scale. At Kew there are several large beds devoted to lilacs, which are attractive and of interest at lilac time. During the other eleven-and-a-bit months of the year you don't really notice that anything is amiss, partly because they are not beside a main path, but mainly because they take up such a small part of Kew as a whole—a mere flea bite compared with the 300-acre site. But in a smaller garden, a lilac collection would represent a much higher proportion of the whole, and for this to be "dead" for eleven months would hardly be acceptable. In fact there's a long list of shrubs that aren't going to look their best placed all together in a collection: *Philadelphus*, *Weigela*, or *Lonicera*, for example, are likely to look exceedingly dreary when out of bloom, and need to have other contrasting plants mixed in with them. Alternatively the collection could be dotted around the whole site. This may be less convenient if you want to compare one with another, but will be better in terms of garden effect.

ROSES

Of all single-genus collections, the rose garden must be the most frequently seen and also the one with the longest and most celebrated history. This is not surprising, bearing in mind the charms of roses. However, considering that there are thousands of different cultivars available, a rose collection aspiring to completeness could be a possibility only for a large garden of national or regional importance. However, a themed collection of roses might be manageable: one could, for example, concentrate on

an institution, such as the garden of a horticultural college or a botanic garden, but are likely to have less appeal in the private garden. Roses are obviously the exception—they are in a class of their own. Then for gardeners on acid soil, rhododendrons and azaleas are a very tempting option. But apart from that there are very few shrubs, despite their various individual attractions, that one would save up and buy a field for. A desire to create a small arboretum is not unknown, but the ambition to plant an extra-large shrubbery seems more-or-less unheard of.

A collection of shrubs all of a single genus (or of varieties of just one species) will tend to highlight the issue of value in relation to size. Because all the shrubs in question will be related to one another, the likelihood is that they will all be fairly similar in form, and flower at more or less the same time of year. This will be fine when they are all in bloom, and hopefully there will be a dazzling display of colour in the garden. But it also means that for the

the 1960s, which I once grew, seems already to be unavailable in Britain. But fashions change, and what goes out of fashion may after a while become fashionable once again.

When it comes to selecting roses, the choice seems unlimited, and new ones continue to stream from the breeders every year. But whether you make a limited collection by period, a collection by type (species, hybrid tea, floribunda, patio, ground cover, etc), or simply grow a few roses you fancy, there will still be the issue of colour to consider, especially if modern roses are chosen. Not all roses blend together. You may or may not like the rose called 'Masquerade'; I do, as it is a "multi"—a mixture of yellow and red—which looks so good with catmint and lavender to cool it down. But it's important to remember that this rose will on no account blend with the soft, mauvey pinks of the old roses. And many of the "salmon pinks" won't blend with the older hint-of-mauve pinks either, because of the trace of yellow they have in them.

ROSE GARDENS

What is most often meant by a rose garden is one in which the dominant plants are roses, blended in with sympathetic perennials, climbers, and occasionally other shrubs, as at the famous English examples of rose gardens at Sissinghurst in Kent and Mottisfont in Hampshire. Completeness is not the issue: all that is aimed at is to create a pleasing garden at rose time, and as far into the other summer months as possible. Even so, such rose gardens are often part of some garden whose overall size is much larger than average and in this context it is perfectly

the Bourbons, or whatever subgroup or historic period took your fancy. It's about time someone made a collection of roses from the 1940s and 1950s. While many of these are still around, there must be many more lingering on in gardens, but abandoned by commerce. 'Eiffel Tower', raised in

acceptable for this particular part of the garden to have only one season of interest.

One of the problems of rose gardens is that roses as plants resent competition by other plants. They hate to be crowded around with vigorous perennials, for example, and respond by sulking and behaving badly. Roses are hungry plants that need feeding, and it is almost impossible to apply a mulch to the surface of ground already covered by other plants. Some gardens open to the public have a rather

sneaky solution: they treat the perennials that grow around their roses as if they were bedding plants, or play musical chairs with them by moving them in and out of a reserve plot—in other words, they generally cheat in ways that are not possible where the only gardener is the garden owner.

However, whether the roses like it or not, a rose garden looks much better when the ground is covered with plants. The combination of bare soil and the prickly knees of roses looks quite hideous, no

matter how beautiful the flowers may be higher up the plant. One solution is to grow taller roses. For instance, I used to associate various low-growing geraniums, hostas, and the yellowy-green *Euphorbia villosa* (a species that is similar to *E. palustris*) with a tall hybrid tea rose with cerise flowers, and the rose seemed reasonably happy. An alternative approach is to be extremely selective about the ground cover you use. At Scotney Castle, in Kent, I've seen pink hybrid teas successfully underplanted with pale

pink *Geranium asphodeloides*, a plant that is not only low-growing, but also spreads out over a wide area from quite a small centre or crown, leaving the ground largely bare in winter for mulching and cultivation.

Picking just one or two roses for a small garden is an impossible task to approach rationally. If I tell you how wonderful 'Renaissance' is, then you will tell me about the merits of various other cultivars. However, on the whole hybrid teas are probably best avoided, because they are such inept mixers. If I had to mention particular roses, I would put in good word for *R. xanthina* 'Canary Bird', because it flowers so early, and *R. glauca*, which has the merit of foliage interest and good habit. Next in value come the rugosas, and after that, the choice of good shrub roses is vast—just don't pick one that's trying to be an old-fashioned rose, but blooms a bit longer. Instead, choose one that reliably covers itself with a succession of flowers, has neat foliage, and doesn't get black spot or mildew. The best plan is to visit gardens where a wide selection of roses is grown, and see which ones look healthy and attractive.

RHODODENDRONS AND AZALEAS

Azaleas are without equal for floral value and are eminently collectable, but are only a possibility if they are grown on lime-free soil. Anyone with an acre or two of lightly shaded acidic woodland to spare could hardly be blamed for giving way to the temptation to collect deciduous azaleas. I don't find the evergreen ones nearly as attractive. All I would ask is that you don't let the labels go missing, as seems to have happened with nine out of ten azalea-etums that one visits. And my second request would be that a little restraint is exercised when it comes to colour. Some people like brilliant orange, but those of us who are sensitive souls would prefer it if you would at least keep the oranges away from the pinks. The beauty of azaleas is that the flowers themselves are often what brick manufacturers call "multis". Within each flower is a range of colours, giving a subtlety to the overall effect. When there are so many lovely creams, pale yellows, and pale pinks,

there is really no need to dazzle the visitor with excessively brash colours. There may be a place for virulent candyfloss pink, but please, not within native-green, deciduous woodland.

Rhododendron collections need huge swathes of space, and even when this is available they are often seen planted too close to each other. All that heavy dark green foliage can be rather overpowering, and in my view about three huge hulks twelve feet (3.5 m) in each direction is about the most one should have to cope with before returning once more to deciduous woodland, or plants of a completely different type. If the same species or cultivar of large rhododendron is repeated, closer planting is possible, as it then begins to look more naturalistic, but walls of endlessly changing colour can get a bit much, however beautiful the flowers. And it's best to lay out the paths in the woodland first, and then plant the rhododendrons to suit the route of the viewer. Don't plant the rhodos first and then have to devise irrationally winding and backtracking paths to enable to visitor to view them.

GROWING PAINS

As with trees (see pages 74–8), there are several ways to cope with the eventual size and growth of shrubs. The obvious solution might seem to be to plant each shrub at a spacing to suit its full-grown size, and this does have much to recommend it. But it also means that for several years there will be large areas of bare soil or chipped bark to look at, and plenty of weeding to do as well. Inevitably, in time these gaps will be seen as tempting homes for plants bought on impulse, thus entirely defeating the object. With

really large plants such as lilacs this is not a sensible approach, and the planting of the blank spaces in between must be approached more methodically. There are several lines of attack.

One approach is to cover the bare soil with perennial ground cover plants, such as lamiums, *Vinca minor* cultivars, symphytums, or *Geranium macrorrhizum*. As the shrubs grow the perennials will slowly be shaded out, but this will be of no consequence, since they were chosen for this purpose and were of no great distinction or rarity. The second approach is to plant dispensable shrubs. Rosemary and purple sage, for example, are neither rare nor expensive, and can easily be pulled out when the time comes. In any case they won't flourish too well once they start being shaded or elbowed out by anything as tall as lilac. The third method is the landscape architect's technique—plant two, three, or perhaps ten or more, of the shrub you actually want. This allows a few weak specimens to die (which assumes that plants in the public or commercial sector will often be poorly maintained), and the survivors will either blend or merge together, or can be thinned out if desired. The final (most common) method is to accept that eventually some moving around of plants is going to have to take place, and take on board the labour and effort involved. As you can see, almost all these solutions require work, all of which sadly proves (to me at least) that the allegedly labour-free shrub garden is a myth.

As for the idea of a shrubbery, this seems to me to be a needlessly limited concept. Just as an arboretum can benefit from having shrubs and perennial ground cover mixed through it, so a shrubbery is greatly improved by not being such a purist concept as "shrubbery" suggests. Nature knows of no such thing. It only knows of habitats, or types of vegetation, which may of course be of various heights. So the occasional tree, some clumps of pampas grass (*Cortaderia*), *Miscanthus*, *Aruncus*, *Camassia*, *Crambe cordifolia*, a sweep of *Calamagrostis*, clumps of *Astilbe rivularis*, or a carpet of some up-market ground cover can all enhance and improve the appearance of a so-called shrubbery.

THE USES OF SHRUBS

In the context of garden-making and "eclectic" collections of plants, one should not plant a shrub just to fill up a space, choosing it at random as one might toss a pebble into a lake. Shrubs have particular uses that other kinds of garden plant (trees, alpines, perennials and so on) cannot provide. One of the most useful ways to employ shrubs is to plant small evergreen ones among perennials to provide foliage interest during the winter months, when all the perennials have died down. Subshrubs such as

BELOW One of the advantages of evergreen shrubs such as *Osmanthus* × *burkwoodii* is that they provide a reticent background for a border of perennials, the bright colours showing up well against the dark green of the shrubs.

BELOW Foliage colour can be an asset in the garden, but too much can become tiresome, especially if the contrasts are too strong, such as yellow foliage against purple.

Jackman's rue (*Ruta graveolens* 'Jackman's Blue'), santolina, ballota, and *Lotus hirsutus* blend very easily, as do artemisias, salvias, and sages. Most of these are evergreen (or ever-grey), and will help to clothe the ground during the winter. Who wants to look out on bare earth for half the year? Sarcococcas are particularly good towards the back of the border. In summer they are hardly noticed, but they come into their own in winter and early spring. Hebes, again, offer a wide range of good varieties to choose from, but perhaps my favourite shrubs for this purpose are the various kinds of phlomis, especially *P. anatolica* 'Lloyd's Variety' and *P. italica*. Most kinds of *Cistus* are also good, and although many of them can get too large, they can be kept in order quite easily. The only down side with *Cistus* is that

after a few years sudden death syndrome can affect them. Just plant another.

Another way in which shrubs can be useful is to provide a dark, evergreen background to more colourful plants. Classic English gardens, with herbaceous borders and plenty of space, often have tall yew hedges behind them, the plain dark green of the yew providing the perfect foil for the bright colours of the flowers in the border. Unfortunately not many of us have the space for a large yew hedge, but the same effect can be achieved by choosing a dark green foliage shrub for the back of the border. As we have seen, size can be a problem, but attractive shrubs such as *Itea ilicifolia* can be restrained easily enough. Other possibilities are osmanthus, *Escallonia* 'Iveyi', and pyracanthas.

BELOW *Juniperus chinensis* 'Kaizuka', the Hollywood juniper, is a classic shrub in the "architectural" category, with stiff dark green branches that sit at an angle of about 45° to the horizontal.

ARCHITECTURAL SHRUBS

The average shrub is vaguely rounded in shape and soft in outline, and therefore comes into the low-impact category of plants, even though it may be quite large in size. However, there are a few shrubs in the "architectural" category, with a much stronger impact. Medium-height varieties of conifers belong here, the classic example being the Hollywood juniper, *Juniperus chinensis* 'Kaizuka', whose branches reach up at almost exactly 45 degrees to the horizontal, giving a quite startling and bold effect. The more common Pfitzer junipers are similar, but not quite so bold. There are also, of course, many vertical conifers of medium height, not quite tall enough to be called trees. These strong characters are useful for creating accent and emphasis in the garden, acting rather like exclamation marks, and they need to be placed where the emphasis is needed, not just dotted at random. They should always be planned in first, at the key points, and the quieter, soft-and-rounded shrubs blended round them later.

Whether you call them shrubs or perennials, yuccas are the winners in the architectural plant category. Dominant, stately, and ferocious-looking, they make the boldest statement of any plant of their size. Mahonias, by contrast, are dark, prickly heavyweights. A large specimen of *Mahonia × media* 'Charity' makes a major statement. A collection of mahonias would be worthwhile (I'm very keen on them), but all that strongly-textured, dark green foliage is best seen in small doses, rather than in rows or clustered in one indigestible clump.

Some architectural shrubs have strong horizontal emphasis, such as *Cornus controversa* 'Variegata' and, on a smaller scale, *Viburnum plicatum* f. *tomentosum* 'Mariesii'. *Buddleja alternifolia*, on the other hand, has long pendulous branches with pale mauve flowers dangling along the stems. *Aralia elata*, sometimes called the devil's walking stick, is somewhere between a shrub and a tree, and has an excellent sculptural outline. This is best appreciated by giving the plant plenty of breathing space—one should plant low ground cover beneath it, rather than crowd it in with plants of a similar height or lumpy shape. *Rhus typhina* (also arguably a small tree) has a similar effect without the thorns, but on the other hand it suckers annoyingly. On the rock garden, *Hebe ochracea* and the other whipcord hebes will give the same effect—a strong statement on a miniature scale.

GOING FOR COVER

When choosing "fillers", or low-impact plants, to go between the major players, the shrubs to look out for are ones that provide effective ground cover. Many shrubs come into this category, from *Rosmarinus officinalis* 'Severn Sea', *Salix helvetica*, and *Cotoneaster congestus* down to carpeters such as junipers and helianthemums. Low-growing conifers such as *Juniperus rigida* subsp. *confertus* will be appreciated during the winter. Heathers are also evergreen, and there are countless *Erica* and *Calluna*

BELOW Many flowering shrubs fill the late spring gap—providing colour and interest between the early spring bulbs and perennials, most of which don't start until midsummer. This is an unusual pale yellow lilac, *Syringa vulgaris* 'Primrose'.

varieties—a good one I saw quite recently was *Calluna vulgaris* 'Alexandra'. Why heathers are currently out of fashion is a mystery. Among slightly taller evergreens, *Lonicera pileata*, *Sarcococca hookeriana* var. *humilis*, *Euonymus fortunei* 'Silver Queen', and *Mahonia repens* are some of the best for this purpose.

It's always worth reminding ourselves that ground cover can be of any height. Some tall shrubs cover the ground and suppress weeds just as well as the low carpeters. However, the smaller kinds are generally the most useful, and with genera such as *Potentilla*, *Spiraea*, or *Cistus* it is a question of discovering which ones are dwarf or prostrate. Among *Potentilla fruticosa* cultivars, 'Beesii' is good, with silvery foliage and bright yellow flowers, but other low-growers include 'Manchu' (white flowers with greyish leaves), 'Dart's Cream', 'Tilford Cream', 'Longacre Variety' (sulphur yellow), 'Tangerine', and 'Pretty Polly' (salmon-pink). Low-growing spiraeas include *S. betulifolia*, *S. japonica* 'Bullata' and 'Magic Carpet', and *S. nipponica* 'Halward's Silver'.

THE LATE SPRING SPLASH

Another way of choosing easy-going low-impact plants is to create a mix that will provide a succession of interest through the year. In the early months, bulbs tend to dominate when it comes to floral interest. From midsummer onwards the main display of perennials begins. But between these two is a gap, and one advantage many shrubs have to offer is their ability to provide spring colour during this period. We have already mentioned lilac (*Syringa*), easy to grow although taking up rather a lot of space. All

lilacs are beautiful in flower, in varying shades of purple, mauve, and even pink, although many of the white ones look unsightly as the flowers die off. Whether this applies to the attractive pale yellow one called 'Primrose', I'm not sure. If only some plant breeder would produce a lilac with a dark, glossy leaf one would feel more kindly towards lilacs when they are out of bloom.

Most *Cornus* species have more style and poise than lilacs do, but again, many are almost tree-sized. One on my Wants List, but too large for my present

BELOW *Cornus kousa*
'Satomi' is a beautiful
specimen shrub for late
spring, with an attractive,
wide-spreading habit. Sadly,
like many excellent shrubs
this shrub is not suitable for
small gardens.

garden, is *Cornus kousa* 'Satomi', with its mass of pink flower bracts elegantly displayed on wide-spreading branches.

Most ceanothus varieties flower during this period, and their colour is unique, the branches covering themselves in wonderful shades of Mediterranean blue (they actually come from west coast America). Many get too large for comfort, however. *Ceanothus cuneatus* var. *rigidus* is small for a ceanothus, but even this reaches 5 feet (1.5 m), compared with the 20 feet (6 m) of *C. arboreus* 'Trewithen Blue'. Ceanothus need sunshine and a warm position, and they don't last forever. After ten or twelve years they can die unexpectedly, but this seems a small price to pay for their display of colour. A ceanothus collection would

really need spreading round the garden, one here, one there, to avoid creating a large blank area once the flowers are over.

The same would apply to a collection of *Philadelphus*, although a few have a longer season of value because of their foliage interest: these are *Philadelphus coronarius* 'Aurea' and 'Variegatus', and *P.* 'Innocence'. These need light shade to avoid scorching of the leaves. Weigelias are another genus that would hardly look their best congregated together, but they have a lot to offer the gardener on alkaline soil, and again the variegated varieties provide more to look at for longer.

Unusual foliage colour can be an asset, but can also be wearisome if used to excess. Yellow, purple,

grey, and blue all at once is overdoing it. But foliage texture is another quality of shrubs worth noting. This is an intermediate feature when it comes to considering the high or low impact of a plant. When putting together plants whose foliage is heavy and dark, one can create a feeling of variety by introducing the light, airy foliage of *Colutea arborescens*, for example, or a caragana, perhaps. Tamarix is another feathery, light-textured plant.

SUMMER-FLOWERING SHRUBS

In very small gardens there seems little point in flowering shrubs for summer display, since at this time of year, anything a shrub can do a perennial can do more compactly. All the same, fuchsias are in a class

of their own. Although they are technically shrubs or subshrubs, most of them are no more woody than a penstemon, and can be used as if they were perennials. There are many first-rate hardy fuchsias, such as *F. magellanica* var. *gracilis* 'Tricolor', *F. magellanica* var. *molinae* 'Sharpitor', and *F.* 'Corallina', 'Margaret', and 'Genii'. There is a vast number of cultivars too tender to be out of doors in temperate gardens, and in any case a collection of bedding-out fuchsias would simply be too overwhelming for any average-sized garden. There comes a point in a monoculture when a garden ceases to be a garden in any normal sense of the word, and becomes, instead, a hobby-zone or an obsession-area. If it consists entirely of fuchsias it will be just that—mind-bending at fuchsia-flowering time, but not a garden in the conventional sense.

The most remarkable of the other late-summer-flowering shrubs are the hydrangeas. As with philadelphus or ceanothus, too many hydrangeas too close together will be liable to create tedium. There are dozens of mop-heads and lace-caps, most forming a rounded (I'm trying to avoid saying lumpy) bush. A whole bed of lumps—sorry, rounded shapes—doesn't look good. But spread them around and they will be fine. All the same, I prefer the larger-leaved species, but these need protection from wind and sun. I was quite bowled over by one I saw recently, *Hydrangea aspera* 'Kawakamii', which sadly is too big for my own garden: this specimen was about ten feet high and eight across (3 m and 2.4 m). *Hydrangea serrata* 'Tiara' is another good one, fortunately a lot smaller, at about three and a half feet (1 m) tall.

BERRIES, FRUITS, AND LEAF COLOUR

Another good reason for growing shrubs in the garden is for the sake of their autumn leaf colour. Acers are in the first rank, but there are also many other contenders. Anyone attempting to create a Japanese maple collection would have my vote—I just envy you all the space you must have, especially when, in about fifteen years' time, people come in their thousands to see your Acer Glade (judging from the pressure on Westonbirt, in Gloucestershire). Do make sure you keep track of the labels. But most of us have room for only one acer. I have 'Ôsakazuki' right by my front door. It has become far too large, blocking the light from one of the windows, and it ought to go. But it's too beautiful—

from the moment the leaves appear until they turn brilliant red in October.

Amelanchiers, cotinus, sumachs (*Rhus*), and more unusual subjects such as *Disanthus*, *Lindera*, and *Gaylussacia*—the list of shrubs with good autumn colour is long, and space here will not permit me to enthuse about them all. Some berberis colour up very well, such as the well-known *B. thunbergii* and its cultivars and forms, but having said that, I must confess that berberis are perhaps my least favourite shrubs, because of the awkward, gawky habit so many have, and the vicious thorns that make pruning them an exercise in self-harm.

Shrubs whose sole claim to fame is their autumn colour are a luxury that can be enjoyed only by gardeners who have plenty of space, although I would

OPPOSITE Anyone
with a small woodland area
at their disposal could be
forgiven for planting an
acer collection. *Acer
palmatum* is graceful
throughout the season,
but in the autumn the rich
colours have no equal.

BELOW LEFT *Euonymus
europaeus* 'Red Cascade', is
possibly the best large shrub
to combine berries and good
autumn foliage.

BELOW RIGHT This
example of *Viburnum
sargentii* var. *puberulum* is
growing at the Sir Harold

Hillier Gardens, Winchester,
Hampshire. It produces good
berries, but these are on a
very large shrub, about
fifteen feet (4.5 m) wide
and high.

put in a word in favour of the small and beautiful *Euonymus alatus*, which admittedly doesn't do a lot until autumn, when it turns an amazing, almost ice-cream pink. But on the whole you will get better value by choosing shrubs that have more than one season of interest. *Rosa virginiana*, for example, turns shades of purple, orange-red, crimson, and yellow in the autumn, but it also has a summer-long display of pink flowers. And it's not that big as species roses go.

Fruits and berries are also a worthwhile asset to the gardening year, lengthening the succession of interest in the garden. Many shrubs have fruits of a sort, but the number that put on a first-class display is fairly small. *Euonymus europaeus* 'Red Cascade' must be among the best, providing autumn colour at

the same time. It's not small, but neither are the other outstanding genera for autumn fruits: *Cotoneaster*, *Pyracantha*, and *Viburnum*. Many of these are excellent shrubs, but again it is hard to see that a one-genus collection of them would have much charm unless broken up with other plants. A few roses have good fruits, such as the rugosas, whose hips (or heps) are quite spectacular, looking like inedible, up-turned, rock-hard tomatoes. Some of the other species roses and their close relations are also good for their hips, such as *Rosa* 'Geranium' (a form of *R. moyesii*), and *R.* 'Wolley-Dod' (which used to be considered a cultivar of *R. villosa*). Again, these roses have the advantage of multi-season garden interest—flowers, good foliage, and then the bristly, apple-shaped fruits.

10
Collecting perennials

PERENNIALS HAVE SO MANY virtues: they're colourful and easy to cultivate, they often flower in the first year of planting, and together they provide a succession of interest during the year. It's also fairly easy to obtain quite unusual and attractive varieties. It's no wonder that they are so desirable and collectable. They are not entirely work-free: they do have to be tidied up now and again, cut down after flowering, divided if they get too big, or restrained if they spread too much. But if plants are like children who can be divided into two kinds, the manageable and the unmanageable, most perennials are definitely in the manageable category.

PLANTING BY NUMBERS

Obviously, perennials are a lot smaller than trees or shrubs, but even so a single-genus collection may need more space than you might think. Even a genus that might not seem very large, such as *Acanthus*, turns out to have thirty species worldwide—and then there are the cultivated varieties and geographical forms. Only two species are commonly grown in temperate gardens, *Acanthus mollis* and *A. spinosus*, but on consulting my current copy of the *RHS Plant Finder*, I find that there are not only six other species available from specialist nurseries, but also twelve cultivars, one subspecies, one botanical variety, one botanical form, three listed under collector's numbers, and two more simply described as "smooth-leaved", or whatever. Altogether making twenty-eight plants—a little more daunting than one might have imagined.

When I began collecting euphorbias, it took a few years before I realized I had to make a decision.

Either I could have a Euphorbia Collection, or I could have a garden in the traditional sense of the word, but not both. I chose to shy away from turning my garden into a one-genus monoculture, but with twice or three times the space the answer might have been different—I could probably have had my cake and eaten it[3].

astilbes, and so on. Further down the alphabet we find: 400 cranesbill geraniums, 750 hostas, and 600 daylilies, and this last number is but a small fraction of the 100,000 cultivated varieties of *Hemerocallis* said to be known to daylily societies. Predictably, nobody has so far volunteered to collect all the bearded *Iris germanica* varieties.

When it comes to collectability, it's a little like finding your life partner—there is someone for everybody. Does anyone want to collect eighty different bergenias, all with similar rounded leaves, and similar flower spikes in shades of red, pink, and white? Yes, somebody does. And that's lucky for the rest of us, who will benefit from the results of the plant searches and comparisons that can be made once they are all growing in the same garden.

Acres may not be required, but all the same an average town or suburban garden won't be enough to hold some genera. Looking in the National Plant Collections Directory issued in Britain by the NCCPG, we find 42 achilleas, 29 aconitums, 150 agapanthus, 46 alchemillas, 200 alliums, 32 Japanese anemones, 100 aquilegias, 350 asters, 185

BELOW The National Collection of penstemons, at Pershore College, Worcestershire. An impressionistic display of colours, showing the range from white through pink and red to burgundy and purple.

BOTTOM Aubrietas with aubrietas may make comparison between cultivars easy, but the overall result is purely functional and cannot be expected to create a pleasing garden picture.

TOGETHER, OR NOT TOGETHER

How to arrange a collection of perennials of one genus is a question that needs serious consideration: the most rational way to keep order is to plant them in neat rows—a long bed about four feet (1.2 m) wide would be ideal, with a clump of each variety or species every three and a half feet (1 m), each kept separate from the next and all carefully and neatly labelled. Alternatively, they could be planted in double-width beds, seven feet (2.1 m) across, to reduce the amount of circulation space used up in paths around the beds. This approach is perfectly

systematic and logical, and makes access, cultivation, and comparison between varieties all very straightforward. However, in the case of many genera, it won't look the least bit interesting, nor will it flatter your collection.

A *Penstemon* collection (for example) wouldn't look too bad set out like this, as the variety of colour would create a pleasing effect, but *Heliopsis* (for instance) would hardly show to advantage, since they would all be yellow and about the same height. Total absence of height would be the problem with any collection of carpeters—imagine the effect of rows of helianthemums, aubrietas, or lamiums. If your chosen plants were acaenas, none of them would be more than an inch (2.5 cm) high. Lack of contrast in form and texture would also be an issue; for instance, geraniums would be all fluff and phormiums all spikes. Another problem might be monotony of foliage colour—for example, in silvery genera such as *Artemisia*, *Anaphalis*, *Dianthus*, and *Helichrysum*.

Eighty *Bergenia* varieties planted in rows would hardly be a thing of beauty either. Although frequently planted in gardens, bergenias don't play a leading role in plant associations, but a secondary or subservient one. They create a strong base line below some other plant that is considered more interesting. A bed devoted to bergenias would be like a Shakespeare play with no leading parts, but made up entirely of servants, confidants, and messengers, and the dramatic effect of a stage-full of such unheroic characters would be almost nil.

If we simply want to be orderly and systematic and compare plant A with plant B, long rows of related plants are an admirable solution, but it's easy

to see that the visual effect is going to be more like an allotment or vegetable garden than a flower garden. The alternative approach is to spread the collection round the garden. This will obviously look much better, and will enable us to appreciate the garden value of the plants in question, but to compare one member of a genus or species with its fellows will not be quite so easy. There is also a risk of swamping the garden with one kind of thing and creating monotony, particularly when the plants in question

are all quite similar in height and form. You need a large garden if you want to dot eighty different bergenias around the place—otherwise it will be all too obvious that you have a curiously one-track mind when it comes to choosing front-row plants for the border. On the other hand, to plant a collection of euphorbias in various places round the garden would be quite reasonable, since they provide a fair range of different shapes, sizes, and habits, even though the flower colour is mostly the same.

BOTH-AND

The ideal solution is to include both approaches. This is called the "Both-And" method (as opposed to that more worrisome approach known as "Either-Or"). At Sizergh Castle, in Cumbria, there's a lushly planted sunken rock garden sited in a large crater-like area behind the house. It has a stream cleverly running through it, and a collection of excellent ferns are grown in the damp, shady places created, some of which are labelled, and some not. What makes this garden successful is that there are not only ferns but also a complete setting of moisture-loving plants such as rodgersias, mimulus, primulas, astilbes, and willow gentians, along with Japanese maples and mature dwarf conifers. Even the ferns in themselves exhibit quite a fair amount of variety, ranging in shape and size from varieties of the massive royal fern, *Osmunda regalis*, reaching four feet (1.2 m) or more, down to the diminutive *Blechnum penna-marina*.

BELOW A border comprised entirely of grasses is rarely successful in design terms. Many grasses are specimen plants, such as the *Stipa gigantea* pictured here, and need a certain amount of breathing space around them in order to be fully appreciated.

BOTTOM A close-up view of one of the cultivars in the border at Bressingham Gardens, pictured on page 110. *Miscanthus sinensis* 'Kaskade'.

In another part of the grounds at Sizergh, not forming part of the ornamental garden proper, a new, dedicated fern border has recently been laid out to take account of the fact that many keen garden visitors would appreciate the opportunity to study the fern collection, plant by plant. So far it looks rather unimpressive, partly because the plants are all young and small compared with their counterparts in the rock garden. But eventually the idea will pay off, especially for fern enthusiasts, of whom I am one.

A similar approach can be seen at Elton Hall in Herefordshire, where there are collections of *Rudbeckia* and *Echinacea*. Many varieties can be seen in the flower borders, but in another part of the garden an orderly collection of both genera is lined out in rows, beautifully labelled.

Not many of us have enough room to display the same plants twice, however. One compromise solution is to plant a specialized collection in beds edged with dwarf box. This gives the scheme some greenery in winter, which is an advantage if the plants being collected are herbaceous, and also provides some structure and "body" in summer. One could imagine the dark green of the box contrasting attractively with the bright colours of a *Phlox* collection, or the silver foliage of different types of *Artemisia*.

At Bressingham Gardens in Norfolk there is a kind of halfway-house approach which works well. An excellent collection of *Miscanthus* has been acquired fairly recently, and these plants are concentrated in just a few beds, but mixed in with the many other perennials for which Bressingham Gardens is deservedly famous. My guess is that about one in

BELOW *Silphium
perfoliatum*, a tall perennial
ideally suited for the back of
the border, where the coarse
and uninteresting greenery
of the lower three-quarters
of the plant can be
effectively hidden.

three of the plants in these beds is a miscanthus. As a result, visitors have the advantage of being able to compare varieties, but in a setting that is both pleasing to the eye and demonstrates a range of good plant associations.

If a fern garden looks best when the ferns are mixed with other moisture-loving plants, the same principle is certainly true of grasses. For some reason, beds or borders devoted entirely to grasses rarely look attractive. There is usually a general lack of flower colour, and insufficient contrast, with too many plants inevitably having narrow, "grassy" leaves and buff-coloured, plume-like flowers. Most of the grass-collection beds I've seen also ignore the fact that some grass species are best treated as feature plants. Grasses such as *Stipa gigantea* (see opposite), *Miscanthus nepalensis*, and *Helictotrichon sempervirens* need their own space and look best when surrounded by plants much lower than they are themselves, so that their shape is shown off to best advantage. When this is ignored we get that "assorted vases on a shelf" look that we have described before. A further problem is that many grasses take most of the season to develop, coming into their own only in late summer. This means that for at least half the year it is hard for the bed to claim that it's decorative or interesting.

WHAT THEY WANT

On the question of placing perennials in the garden, there can easily be a mismatch between the places where we want to grow them, and what their needs are as plants, and this applies whether we are planting them in a general way in the garden, or planting

out a specialist collection. In a large garden there is no problem in keeping perennials happy, but in the small garden it's not so easy. Many perennials are plants of the prairies, grasslands, and meadows, accustomed in the wild to open aspect, full sun, and no competition from the greedy roots of shrubs or trees, and this seems to apply particularly to the brightly coloured and floriferous kinds. The snag is that in a town or suburban garden the planting tends to be against the boundaries, with the lawn in the centre and a tree or two in the corners to provide height and screening. This scenario creates a lawn that is very usable for children and adults, and from a visual point of view, the smooth surface contrasts well with the busy shapes of plants around it. But if the borders are too narrow and shaded by the boundaries, with the soil shared by the roots of trees and hedges, this won't provide the best conditions for perennials.

Ideally, the best place to plant perennials is as far away from any boundary fences and hedges as possible. Boundaries inevitably cast some shade for part of the day, and this will tend to make the taller perennials, such as macleayas, flop forward, no matter what the orientation of the border. Even on a sunny wall, a background of woody climbers or shrubs will create competition for light and moisture that perennials will resent.

If the garden exists only to grow plants and be of horticultural interest, there is no difficulty. We can create an island of perennials in mid-garden with paths at the edges. But if there is a demand for family-friendly space, with a lawn, or paving to provide a large sitting area, a conflict of interests arises, and there is no simple way to square this particular circle. It's the age-old question—which is more important, the garden or the plants?

It's easy to forget that the traditional herbaceous border, as found in England's stately homes, was long, but also very deep—up to twenty feet (6 m) from front to back in some cases—which meant that most of the plants were well away from the fence or hedge behind them. In fact the border often had a path at the back that allowed for a yew hedge to be pruned without disturbing the plants. It also gave access to the plants at the back of the border, kept them away from competing roots, and brought the tall perennials into the light, which enabled them to grow straight without staking.

Another effect of narrow borders is to restrict us as to the size and height of plant we can grow. A border that is six feet deep (1.8 m) might seem to be reasonably generous in a town garden, but if you want to grow perennials in an ideal manner this would only provide enough depth for two rows of different plants, supposing them to be perennials of average proportions, and also assuming they are grown with enough space to develop into good healthy specimens, not squeezed uncomfortably by their neighbours. (Of course, many plant addicts are incorrigible squeezers-in.)

A border about six feet (1.8 m) deep would allow for a lowish perennial at the front, with a medium-height plant placed behind. In other words, some tall perennials would be unsatisfactory in this situation, as many of them don't look attractive if their lower parts are exposed (I know the feeling). *Macleaya cordata* would be fine because it has good foliage all the way down the plant. But with a phlox, which is not that tall as perennials go, everything happens at the top of the plant. Below the top ten inches (25 cm) there is nothing but undistinguished greenery, and it is much better to have another plant positioned in front to hide all those uninteresting leaves. There are numerous perennials that are much taller than phlox and these definitely need something else in front of them: *Aconitum*, *Aster novae-angliae*, delphiniums, *Echinops*, *Euphorbia villosa*, *Helianthus*, inulas, lysimachias, monardas, tall rudbeckias, sanguisorbas, silphiums, and *Veronicastrum virginicum*. Most of these need to be at the back of a three-row-deep border, and planted in good-sized clumps, to prevent them looking too lamp-post-like. In which case the border needs to be more like nine to ten feet (2.7 to 3 m) deep.

On the other hand, there are some perennials of medium height that make good candidates for front-row positions. For instance, the flower spikes of *Acanthus* are fairly tall, but nevertheless the plant deserves a front-of-border position to show off the excellent ensemble of bold foliage and dramatic flowers: anything placed in front of it would spoil the effect. Hosta foliage also asks to be seen to advantage, and the same "whole-plant value" applies to *Euphorbia characias*, *Helleborus argutifolius*, *Matteuccia struthiopteris*, specimen grasses, and *Perovskia*. Other substantial perennials that are good enough for the front row are Japanese anemones,

the shorter daylilies (*Hemerocallis*), bearded irises, *Aruncus dioicus*, rodgersias, and *Salvia × superba*.

Most perennials look best in a clump of reasonable size. In an ideal world one should plant at least three plants of the same kind together. With many perennials a clump a lot taller than it is wide looks uncomfortable. A good rule is that a clump should be three times as wide as it is high. In other words, the taller a perennial is, the more of it you need if the clump is to look strong and balanced. A smidgeon of a plant squeezed in looks as though it has been stunted by lack of care, or on the other hand it may be always pushing its elbows uncomfortably against its neighbours. Of course, you won't want to know this if you, like me, are trying to grow more plants than your garden can sensibly hold. In a small garden, we have to live with the constant need to strike a balance between size (how big each plant is) and variety (how many different ones we can have).

Perennials need a reasonable amount of breathing space around them if the result is going to look comfortable. The best approach is to place three or four plants of the same kind close enough for them to mingle together, with a wider gap between the group and the adjoining plant. A rough guide is to have twelve inches (30 cm) between the plants of the same kind and eighteen inches (45 cm) between one group and the next, although this has to be varied depending on the plant in question. The best and most conscientious gardeners keep a notebook, and one of the most useful notes you can make in its pages is a record (at flowering time, or whenever) of adjustments that need to be made to plant spacings, so that you don't forget in the autumn.

The idea of having gaps in the border is anathema to many gardeners, and this is one of the advantages of the "carpet garden".

THE CARPET GARDEN

How much work do we actually want to do in the garden? Do we really want to be the slaves of a self-inflicted horticultural work ethic? It's possible—you can have a good garden and also have time to lie back in a chair reading the paper, chatting, or even (heaven forfend) just sit there admiring the results of your own handiwork. If the idea of a moment or two of idleness does secretly appeal to you (climate and spouse permitting) then serious attention should be given to the attractions of ground-cover plants.

One helpful way to approach ground cover is to think of your bed as a carpet (if that doesn't sound seriously confusing). This method is particularly useful when you are making a new border. Once the bed has been prepared and perennial weeds have been eliminated, the next stage is to plant the whole border with a wall-to-wall carpet of small, low, yielding, non-aggressive, easy-to-remove, weed-smothering plants. It's true that only a few ground-cover plants fit all of these requirements—on the contrary, the chief merit of many is that they are tough and difficult to kill. Two ideal examples for our purposes here are *Geranium macrorrhizum* (and its cultivars), and *G.* × *cantabrigiense* 'Biokovo'. Into this new carpet go the plants you really want.

Many perennials are tough enough to establish themselves among this gentle and accommodating kind of cover. *Hemerocallis*, peonies, kniphofias, phloxes, penstemons, and perennial asters will simply ignore the small, push-over leaves around their feet and get on with the business of growing and flowering. More delicate subjects will need to go into a different kind of border, where they can be cosseted. (Monardas, for example, I find are a bit hesitant when they first come up in the spring.)

The traditional horticulturist may complain that having plants perpetually covering the border will

BELOW One of the best plants for making a "carpet garden" is low-growing *Geranium* × *cantabrigiense* 'Biokovo', a neat grower, not too high, with foliage that often overwinters and white flowers in midsummer.

prevent you from working any goodness into it during the winter months—a good layer of muck, manure, compost, or whatever—to keep the soil fertile and the plants at peak performance. The compensation is that you will be forced to save yourself all that tedious labour and make do with sprinkling fish and bone meal over it instead—almost as good, and much less bother.

The foliage of both of our ideal plants for this purpose (*Geranium macrorrhizum* and *G.* × *cantabrigiense* 'Biokovo') is neat, interesting, and well behaved, and persists through the winter—unless the weather is particularly severe. Sun or shade will do, although light shade is probably best. If you handle the leaves of *G. macrorrhizum* you will find that they are scented, pleasantly in my view, although opinions differ on this. One great advantage of these two geraniums is that they are easy to propagate: any trailing stem can be broken off and it will take. Three or more stems can be put into a small pot at any time during the summer, and will make a plantable plant within just a couple of weeks. In the autumn you don't even have to pot them up—you can put them straight into the ground where you want them, as long as you keep them watered while they establish.

The flowers of *G. macrorrhizum* and its cultivars appear in early summer, in shades of pink and white, with slight variations of height. The best in my experience are 'Bevan's Variety' and 'Album'. However, 'Czakor' is allegedly an improvement on 'Bevan's', 'White-Ness' is whiter than 'Album', 'Ingwersen's Variety' is pink, while 'Spessart' has a pink and white effect. 'Biokovo' is the most useful of the *G.* × *cantabrigiense* cultivars, in my view, not being as tall as 'Cambridge', which is the most common pink form. 'St Ola' is is very similar to 'Biokovo'.

You could try other geraniums to provide this carpet effect, such as *G. dalmaticum*, which would work well on a smaller, rock-garden scale, since it is very low-growing. Other possibilities are *G. asphodeloides*, *G. himalayense* cultivars, *G. sanguineum* cultivars, *G.* 'Orkney Pink', and *G.* 'Little Gem', but I am doubtful whether any of them would be as good as 'Biokovo', or "*Ger. mac.*", as its frequent users

call it. These other geraniums have a slightly different growth habit that is not so ideal, and the foliage of some of them looks poor by the end of the year.

Most lamiums also fall into this small category of yielding carpeters. The best known is the one formerly labelled *L. galeobdolon* 'Variegatum', now var. *montanum* 'Florentinum'. Happy in shade, it spreads vigorously, but is nowhere in the same league as the geraniums when it comes to flowers. 'Silver Angel' is just as fast a spreader, but 'Silberteppich' ("silver carpet") and 'Hermann's Pride' are slower and prettier. There are also several worthwhile forms of *Lamium maculatum*, including 'White Nancy', 'Beacon Silver', 'Cannon's Gold', 'Chequers', Golden Anniversary', 'James Boyd Parselle', and 'Pink Pewter'.

Waldsteinia ternata, with its strawberry-like leaves, and the little grey-leaved *Potentilla alba* can also be used as a ground-covering carpet. They are not exciting, but that is not their role here. Acaenas could be tried in full sun, but they need some nursing in the first instance to create effective cover. Totally prostrate, their leading shoots have to be nipped to encourage the plant to cover one piece of ground before it tries to run on to the next. They come in unusual shades of pewter, purpley-grey, or khaki-brown. An equally prostrate shade-lover is *Lysimachia japonica* var. *minutissima*, a ground-hugger only an inch (2.5 cm) high. *Galium* (formerly *Asperula*) *odoratum* would be "part-able" enough for our needs, letting other taller plants through; this is a delicate little shade-lover, four or five inches (10 or 12 cm) high, which can be invasive in some situations. *Adiantum venustum*, a useful slow-creeping, ground-covering fern, six inches (15 cm) high, is particularly appropriate (obviously) in the fern border.

Other possibilities that could be experimented with are ajugas, antennarias, *Erodium manescaui*, *Iberis*, *Persicaria affinis*, and the shade-lovers *Asarum europaeum*, *Mitella breweri*, and *Omphalodes verna*. I have seen *Aegopodium podagraria* 'Variegatum' used effectively as a border carpeter, but since this is the variegated form of the noxious weed ground elder (or bishop's weed), it is exceedingly vigorous, and you try it at your peril. Certainly the plants it surrounds need to be extra tough, but it would be perfectly safe below shrubs, or the fend-for-itself type of perennial (of which there are plenty) such as *Aruncus*, *Telekia* (formerly *Buphthalmum*) *speciosa*, camassias, *Campanula latiloba*, *Centaurea macrocephala*, pampas grass (*Cortaderia*), daylilies (*Hemerocallis*), *Dictamnus albus*, eupatoriums, *Euphorbia palustris*, filipendulas, *Geranium*

psilostemon, inulas, miscanthus, peonies, persicarias, and *Sinacalia tangutica*.

The term "ground-cover plant" implies not only the tendency to cover a local patch of ground, but also the ability to keep weeds at bay. A wide selection of much taller perennials can also do this, of course, far more than would be suitable for the carpeting technique just described, and far too many to list, except in another book. Some, like *Trifolium repens* 'Green Ice', have interesting foliage colour, but you could also get ground cover of sorts from *Acanthus*, *Acorus*, *Agapanthus*, *Alchemilla*, *Arabis*, *Anemone* × *hybrida*, *Aubrieta*, *Artemisia*, *Astilbe*, *Bergenia*, *Brunnera*, *Carex*, *Ceratostigma*, *Coreopsis*—you get the idea. Many of these are well worth growing because we admire them for their own sake, rather than for their quasi-utilitarian ground-covering abilities. It is to the admirable qualities of various kinds of perennials that we now turn.

11
Choosing perennials

ALTHOUGH PLANT-LOVERS are in the main reasonably enterprising people, comparatively few are likely to be brave enough to take on a one-genus collection of perennials in a formal way. To be a "collection-holder" sounds a slightly daunting role to have in life. Nevertheless, most keen gardeners will want to grow a wide selection of perennials in their gardens, and the specialist collector will no doubt want to grow many other perennials besides those in the favoured genus. With a vast range of perennials at our disposal, how can anyone choose between their various attractions, or make a rational selection for the garden? It is easy to be seduced by the beauty of certain individual flowers. Some gardeners may be persuaded by the charm of a well-thought-out colour scheme. Many of us begin quite simply by accepting whatever plants friends and acquaintances recommend, or thrust into our hands.

DRAMATIS PERSONAE

The best way to approach a planting scheme, in my view, is to consider which plants we want to be the major players in the garden. What are the bold and dramatic effects we want to create? "Architectural plants" are not necessarily shrubs; the label also applies to the strong characters of the perennial world. Spiky plants like phormiums and yuccas are the archetypal examples of strong characters in the perennial garden, plants with the highest of "high impact ratings". With their fierce looks and dramatic outlines they have all the virtues and fatal flaws of tragic heroes and heroines.

In contrast to these major players, many good perennials make little contribution to the garden as a

OPPOSITE Silvery biennial
Onopordum acanthium
makes a striking architectural
plant, up to eight feet
(2.4 m) high, beautiful in
midsummer when the sun
catches it.

BELOW LEFT Spiky
phormiums are strong
characters in the garden,
with high impact.

BELOW RIGHT *Erodium*
'Stephanie' may be a pretty
little plant, but with its small
size and rounded shape it
will never be a major player.

BOTTOM In spite of its
impressive name, *Geranium
sessiliflorum* subsp. *novae-
zelandiae* 'Nigricans' is a
reticent plant, interesting
close to, but virtually invisible
from ten feet (2.5m) away.
Sadly it's the same colour as
the soil it's planted in.

whole even though they are good when seen close to. Generally, the smaller the plant, the less the impact. Low-growing plants such as ajugas, and a hundred and one other charming tiny tots, can never be expected to contribute anything much to the greater garden picture, however much we may like and admire them for themselves. Plants such as *Alchemilla conjuncta*, erodiums, and dianthus play their part in the garden, but it's a small one: the flowers don't exactly come out and hit you, and in terms of form, many of these plants don't really have much shape. When we place them in the garden we have to remember that they're "fillers", not plants with garden impact.

Anything small and purple- or brown-leaved is likely to be an example of a plant that may be attractive or unusual in itself, but is likely to disappear from view once you stand back from the border. If you want a completely invisible plant, try *Ranunculus ficaria* 'Brazen Hussy'. No height, no interest, no foliage colour—personally I'd be just as happy

buying a pot of compost. I was once detected by a kind nursery owner photographing 'Brazen Hussy' (I can't think why), and I was promptly led with great enthusiasm to another celandine, 'Old Master', and told in effusive terms that its leaves were not only just as brown, but also attractively mottled. We eventually found the said patch of brown, and after getting down on my knees beside the plant (known in the manual as the plant-worshipping position),

LEFT This interesting
architectural umbellifer
from Southern Greece,
*Molopospermum
peloponnesiacum*, is
known to its friends as
"Molly the Greek".

yes, it was true; the leaves of this almost invisible plant were indeed very slightly mottled.

THE LEAD PLAYERS

Who, then, are the candidates for the major roles in our planting schemes, the high-impact perennials around which we will arrange the lesser plants? Many high-impact perennials are tall, not surprisingly, since these are plants that draw attention to themselves. The cardoon (*Cynara cardunculus*), for example, with its attractively arching silvery leaves, is six to ten feet (2 to 3 m) or more high. Other dramatic perennials include *Eryngium pandanifolium*, a giant among South American sea hollies; the taller globe thistles (*Echinops*); and various unusual umbellifers, such as *Molopospermum peloponnesiacum* ("Molly the Greek"), *Opopanax chironium*, and *Ferula communis*.

Several extremely striking plants for the border are biennial and, since they don't have a chapter of their own, had better be included here: the magnificent *Heracleum mantegazzianum*, big enough to decorate the Royal Albert Hall (as Graham Stuart Thomas says), and coming complete with a government health warning, in case you are allergic to its sap; *Angelica archangelica*, another stately member of the umbellifer family; *Onopordum acanthium*, the so-called Scotch thistle; and verbascums, especially *V. olympicum*.

Perennials with large or imposing foliage also belong in this high-impact category, and well deserve a share of the limelight. *Macleaya cordata*, the plume poppy, with its lovely wavy edged, grey-green foliage, is one of my favourites, as is *Acanthus mollis*. Other notable stars of the show include *Aruncus dioicus*, astelias, *Aralia cachemirica*, *Darmera peltata*, *Euphorbia mellifera*, *Sinacalia tangutica*, pampas grass (*Cortaderia selloana*), the Himalayan bracken relative *Pteris wallichiana*, and *Osmunda regalis*, the royal fern.

On a slightly smaller scale, but still with that sense of "presence", we find *Euphorbia characias*, filipendulas, *Helleborus argutifolius*, *Kirengeshoma palmata*, *Kniphofia caulescens*, *Rodgersia podophylla*, and *Zantedeschia aethiopica*; grasses such as *Deschampsia cespitosa* cultivars, moisture-loving *Schoenoplectus lacustris* subsp. *tabernaemontani* 'Albescens', *Stipa gigantea*, *Chionochloa rubra*, and *Calamagrostis* × *acutiflora* 'Karl Foerster'; and ferns such as *Matteuccia struthiopteris*, *Blechnum chilense*, and many excellent *Polystichum setiferum* varieties in the Divisilobum and Bevis groups.

BELOW This tall, high-impact fern, *Pteris wallichianum*, is from the Himalayas and is seen growing here at the RHS Garden, Rosemoor, in Devon. It is a relation of bracken, which grows prolifically in many wild parts of Britain.

BOTTOM Even a fairly low-growing plant, such as *Ophiopogon jaburan* 'Vittatus', can have "presence" and look better when it isn't crowded in by other plants of equal height.

other hand, there are medium-sized to quite small plants that have "presence", and therefore require a reasonable amount of space around them. Examples are hostas, which may not be large but still benefit from being allowed to show off their shape and outline. Many other ferns and perennials that grow from a strongly central crown or rosette need the same treatment, for example: celmisias, *Crambe maritima*, *Ophiopogon jaburan* 'Vittatus', grasses such as the shorter pennisetums and *Festuca mairei*, and sedges such as the brown *Carex buchananii* and *C. oshimensis* 'Evergold'. All of these appreciate being considered as mini-specimen plants. Some look good growing in gravel, or at least with nothing taller than an acaena.

THE MIDDLE CLASSES

Every good garden needs a few high-impact plants, strong-charactered or architectural, call them what you will, but it would be no good cramming the garden with too many of them: the result would far too busy and hectic, a bit like having too many noisy extroverts at a party. You need a few quieter people (like me) to balance things out a bit.

But a whole range of perennials lies somewhere between the two extremes of yuccas on the one hand, and alchemillas and acaenas on the other. For instance, there are plants which are only temporarily dominating. Miscanthus, for example, have high impact from midsummer onwards, even into November, with their tall, graceful habit and arching plumes, but for the rest of the year they are hardly part of the action: in winter they are resting and look a mess even if you try to tidy them up, and then from

The size of a plant and its quality are not the same thing, of course, and several very tall perennials may be large, but are also rather coarse, such as some *Helianthus*, silphiums, elecampane (*Inula helenium*), and the giant reed grass *Arundo donax*. On the

spring to summer they are busy growing. Many a kniphofia is in the same league: nothing could be more bold and assertive than the set of bright exclamation marks in the border when they are in full flower. But they will only be their bold and assertive selves for six weeks or so. Umbellifers, some of which were mentioned earlier, have their long run of drama, but later on they take early retirement and some even leave a gap in the border.

Other perennials can be described as having "medium impact" within the garden because of their foliage interest. Devotees of foliage plants rightly point out that flowers may come and go, but leaves are always with us. But moderation is needed, to my way of thinking: if you overplay the foliage card your garden will have forty shades of green, silver, purple, and brown in midsummer, while everyone else's will be dazzling their owners with a much more brilliant array of colours.

Another issue is that it's entirely possible to have too many different foliage colours together. This can look a bit kitsch: *Hosta* 'Hadspen Blue' next to Bowles' golden sedge (*Carex elata* 'Aurea') makes me cringe, I confess. In my own garden I admit to having *Carex oshimensis* 'Evergold' next to *Berberis thunbergii* 'Atropurpurea Nana', but this is a bit naff, I've now decided, and it's time I did something about correcting it.

Silver plants look splendid in the summer sunlight: the photographs prove it. But spare a thought for how dreary they will look in the grey and sunless depths of winter. Artemisias and their ilk are very valuable in the garden, but don't overdo it—an all-silver border might be excessive.

Variegated foliage is very useful for brightening up shady areas—in fact plants with white-variegated leaves are often best in shade, whereas yellow variegation seems best in the sun. Silvery pulmonarias like 'Diana Clare', variegated brunneras such as *B. macrophylla* 'Jack Frost', or the interestingly marked forms of *Impatiens omeiana* also liven up darkish corners. In shade, blue and glaucous foliage seems out of place; to my mind, blue foliage is best blended in with the silvers, as it looks more at home in the sunlight. There are several good dicentras with

blue, ferny foliage, but I don't rate the little blue festucas very highly, although there are several other good blue grasses, such as *Elymus magellanicus*.

Not many perennials (fortunately, in my view) have brown or purple foliage. *Lysimachia ciliata* 'Firecracker' is the most effective if you insist on having a big patch of purple/brown about two feet (60 cm) high. But it's a terrible runner. However, *Rheum palmatum* 'Atrosanguineum' is in a different league, as a magnificent and huge foliage plant, needing shelter and moisture, dying down (messily) in winter. *Lobelia* 'Queen Victoria' is another lover of damp places, with the most startlingly brilliant red of any flowers outside of a poppy—the brown leaves actually help to calm it down a bit. Apart from this, there are, of course, dozens of heucheras which I will leave heucherophiles to dote upon.

A foliage quality often ignored by gardeners is that of texture. Many dicentras have delicate leaves that beautifully complement the flowers—'Stuart Boothman' is particularly good in this respect. The leaves of *Crambe cordifolia*, on the other hand, are dark green, coarse, and leathery. Those of bergenias are smooth and glossy. Limoniums, or sea lavenders, are a mass of delicate featheriness when in bloom. For a mass of prickly, metallic silveriness there is nothing to touch the Mediterranean eryngiums: *E.* × *tripartitum*, for example, or *E.* 'Jos Eijking', but there are many more.

CAMEO ROLES

Once you categorize perennials by their impact rating in the garden, a wide range of diminutive plants such as small cranesbill geraniums or purple-leaved heucheras find themselves at the low-impact end of the scale. Beyond that you venture into the world of cute little Lilliputians, which deserve to play their part on a much smaller stage, in a trough or raised bed (see the chapter on alpines on pages 150–7), instead of being lost in the border.

But there is another category of plant, typified by the toad-lilies, or *Tricyrtis* species. Get close up to them and nobody could fail to be impressed by their extraordinary flowers: oddly shaped, and spotted in exotic shades of purple, maroon, and brown. But sadly the plant as a whole, although quite large, is so dull as to deserve only a very unimportant corner in the garden. (And as luck would have it, they are shade-tolerant.)

Arisaemas are another instance of a plant that is slightly difficult to handle in the garden. With many of these you have to get into the plant-worshipping pose to see their extraordinary—some would say quite weird—hooded flowers. Sometimes you even have to poke among the leaves before you find

them—although it's worth it, I promise. But at least (unlike a *Tricyrtis*) their leaves have considerable merit, a little like a cluster of mini-palm trees, up to about two feet (60 cm) tall. However, they aren't exactly prompt in coming up. In many cases you won't see a leaf until June, but you could plant a few shade-loving bulbs around them. Pinellias are somewhat similar, but not always as good.

LONG BLOOMERS

Once the high-impact plants are in position, a range of "fillers" will be needed to go in between them. First are the ground-cover plants discussed in the section on the "carpet garden" in Chapter 10 (see pages 120–3). Next are the perennials that flower for a long period, plants which will give us good value for the space they occupy—they may not be distinctive in form, but they may flower for weeks on end. The third category contains plants that will provide a succession of interest throughout the seasons of the year.

There is only one perennial I have ever heard of that blooms perpetually, and this is a euphorbia from Sicily called *E. ceratocarpa*. It will only do this given certain temperature limitations (about Zones 8–9), but it certainly bloomed non-stop in my own garden for several years until we had a particularly hard winter. Two and a half feet (75 cm) high and three and a half (1 m) across, it covers itself with a good display of euphorbia-yellow flowers. Rounded in shape and mild in its colour, it's a typical "filler". *Euphorbia ceratocarpa* isn't the finest euphorbia in the pack, but you can't have everything. Other euphorbias that bloom for a long time include the

dry-shade stalwart *E. robbiae* (ten weeks) and *E. cyparissias* (eight weeks). In addition, *Euphorbia characias* and *E. palustris* have a long period of what might be called "evolving interest"—in other words, it takes time for the flowers to develop, in late winter or early spring respectively, and this process can be watched on a day-to-day basis for many weeks.

Other perennials offering non-stop performance for many weeks are the perennial wallflowers, such as *Erysimum* 'Bowles' Mauve', 'John Codrington' and many more. For several years I had *Malva*

moschata f. *alba*, which blooms from late spring through until late summer, with pure white, typical mallow flowers on a plant standing about eighteen inches (45 cm) high. Eventually it disappeared—but I am not to blame, apparently, as it is short-lived, and I should have kept the seedling that I had, instead of giving it away.

From midsummer onwards penstemons are a huge asset to the garden, flowering on until the autumn. The range is huge, but the frequently seen 'Andenken an Friedrich Hahn' (also known as 'Garnet'), 'Hidcote Pink', and 'Evelyn' are all good. My

own particular list of favourites includes 'Schoen-holzeri' (Chinese red and alias 'Firebird'), 'Fujiyama' (white tinged with pink), 'Raven' (deep burgundy), 'Midnight' (imperial purple), and 'Mother of Pearl' (opal with a mauve throat). But I am open to be persuaded that other cultivars are just as good—such as 'Elmley' (deep pink), 'Patio Wine' (pink), 'Apricot Cottage' (lavender pink), 'Port Wine', 'Beckford' (white with a hint of pink), and 'Rich Ruby'. One of the great things about growing penstemons is how easy they are to propagate, and there is no reason why you should not have enormous impressionistic clouds of penstemons in your borders. Try planting five different varieties together, closer than they ought to be, so that all the flowers intermingle to form an extraordinary, apparently multi-coloured plant.

Persicaria amplexicaulis 'Atrosanguinea' also has the advantage of a long flowering period, with erect crimson spikes from midsummer until the first frosts arrive. 'Firetail' is another good variety, although 'Alba' is disappointing. Persicarias are not in the first rank when it comes to the flowers themselves, but it is unreasonable to expect everything from one plant, and they also tend to demand elbow-room unless they are regularly restrained. "Good for the wild garden" gives you the hint. *Persicaria campanulata* also flowers over a long period, in pale pink, again rather vigorous, particularly on the damp soil it prefers, though it can look sophisticatedly challenged among more refined plants.

Other good time-value perennials include *Acanthus* (again), and *Coreopsis verticillata*, which will give you yellow daisy flowers on delicate sprays for several months. Solidagos also flower for ages, supposing you like them—they seem very weedy to me. However, their admirers rightly point to the merits of the shorter and paler varieties, such as 'Golden-mosa', 'Ledsham', and the related hybrids × *Solidaster luteus* 'Lemore' and 'Super'. A few heleniums flower come into this category, in particular 'Wyndley', 'Dunkelpracht', and 'Moerheim Beauty'. As a camera-carrying garden visitor I find heleniums photograph wonderfully, and seem to be underrated plants to me. But don't plant them in wet clay.

To carry you right through the autumn season, a group of Michaelmas daisy relatives will provide good value: these are *Aster thomsonii* 'Nanus', and *A.* × *frikartii* 'Mönch' and 'Flora's Delight'. Their colour is not as startling as many other asters but what you lose in colour brilliance you gain in weeks of display. Several other asters perform for quite a long time, particularly the *A. amellus* varieties. On

the other hand, the shortest-lived are the colourful, and often mildew-ridden *A. novi-belgii* varieties.

A FLOWER FOR EVERY DAY

High-impact plants and long-lasting floral interest can lay the foundations for any planting scheme, but something more is needed. No true gardener wants a static, vacuum-the-patio type of garden, fixed once and for all, and that's it. Many of the most desirable perennials have only a relatively brief moment of glory, yet they still deserve to be included in our company of players. What we want is to be able to go out every day and tour the estate (whether big or small) and see what our little protégées are getting up to. What's new? Who's flaunting it in the bed or border, what's coming up, opening its petals, or tempting us with its fruit or scent, what needs some tender loving care? A year-full of performing plants is what we want. A complete list of the year's perennials would make a book in itself, but let me remind you of just a few of the best.

As the shortest day of the year approaches, in mild districts, *Euphorbia rigida* will start to flower. After Christmas come the hellebores, followed in succession by the pulmonarias, the bergenias, *Hacquetia epipactis*, vincas, pulsatillas, brunneras, epimediums, dwarf phlox, erysimums, doronicums, euphorbias, dicentras, and violas. The only word of caution for owners of small gardens is to bear in mind that if the beds are filled with early-flowering plants like hellebores and pulmonarias, there will be less space for brighter perennials later on—so don't be a Helle Bore, don't get carried away.

Few of the plants that provide interest during the darker months are as impressive as the summer perennials. To give that succession of interest, every garden needs a handful of irises, a peony (or two), and as many geraniums as is reasonable, and after that the stream of perennials is in full flood and it is a question of choosing favourites. Phloxes, campanulas, astrantias, astilbes, and delphiniums all have their devotees, but personally I'm a kniphofia fan, I'm hooked on *Hemerocallis*, I'm persuaded by penstemons, echinaceas, rudbeckias, and then the genus *Heliopsis* is surely underrated, and then—there are so many, you'll have choose for yourself ... The high season of perennials is like the curve of a graph that takes off at the end of spring, peaks in high summer, and tails off again in autumn. Only then does the display begin to falter as the last members of the genus *Aster* finish flowering, followed by the chrysanthemums, until (in mild districts) *Euphorbia rigida* flowers once again.

WINTERS OF PERENNIAL CONTENT

Between late autumn and late spring it would be easy to give up on the perennial garden, and accept that, with many herbaceous plants, a view over bare patches of earth must be our lot. However, there is a small group of perennials that can come to the rescue here because of their over-wintering stems. The

epimediums, kniphofias, and ferns. These are all use-ful plants in providing green "cover" during winter. Personally I think it's very important to know what the winter foliage effect of a plant is, but this is very poorly documented. If you can choose between sev-eral bergenias (again) or between several kniphofias of apparently equal merit, you should really choose the one with the best winter foliage. Sadly you won't find this in any of the gardening books. Experts on the winter garden will tell you all about hellebores and hamamelis, but they won't say which perennials have a neat green tuft of leaves all winter, which dis-appear altogether, and which leave a raggedy looking mess behind them.

Another feature not to be overlooked is known as "beautiful death syndrome". This takes into account the fact that some plants go on looking interesting, if not actually beautiful, long after the flowers are strictly over. A good example of the syndrome is *Leuzea rhapontica* (formerly a *Centaurea*), with knapweed heads, which stay looking good for a good week or two after the flowers are over. Several *Ligularia* and *Agastache* species also fall into this category, and other plants that are worth thinking about before you cut them down include inulas, eupatoriums, and veronicastrums.

But this idea has to be exercised with a degree of moderation. In some gardens, I've seen large parts of the display begin to look ragged and messy by late summer, due to an excessively rigorous adherence to the ideology that nothing must be cut down until late autumn, and the visitor comes away murmuring that he could have stayed at home and looked at his own muddles, for free.

classic example is *Euphorbia characias*, though I may be biased about its many merits. There are many others: bergenias has already been mentioned, dianthus, South American eryngiums, *Euphorbia amygdaloides* and *E. × martini*, *E. robbiae*, and *E. myrsinites*; hellebores, heucheras, liriopes, penste-mons, and *Stachys byzantina*, along with several

12
Bulbs

Bulbs have quite specific needs, differing in many respects from those of other plants, and as a result it's not always easy to decide on the best position for them in the garden. A place in the mixed border is not always suitable, for example, since there are many bulbs that are not up to the task of defending their corner against vigorous or unyielding shrubs and leafy perennials—and not everyone has the time and patience to lift them after they've flowered and replant them again in the autumn. There are some types of bulb that can be happily left to fend for themselves in rough grass or an old orchard. We could plant them in the lawn—but then there's the worry that it will look an awful mess for several months.

HOW, WHEN, AND WHERE

The enthusiast might think that it would better for bulbs to have stand-alone, purpose-made beds all to themselves. As a general rule, the greater the dedication of the gardener to a particular plant or group of plants, the more likely it is that they will be given special treatment. In the case of bulbs, the result of this very focused approach can take on the aspect of a serious and unusual hobby, rather than ornamental gardening as we know it. Luckily this need not apply to every kind of bulbous plant: quite a few of them have a slightly ambiguous status, being claimed by books on perennials as well as by books on bulbs—crocosmias, for example. We shall therefore explore the various and best ways of growing bulbs, corms, and so forth, whether in the border, in grass, in a meadow, in gravel borders, or in raised beds.

LARGESSE

Anyone wanting to make a single-genus collection of bulbs will find that some genera are quite large, and have also produced a great number of varieties. There are, for example, some 1,500 different Narcissus readily available in Britain at the moment, and this is only a fraction of what a dedicated collector could acquire. One collection, open to view[4], boasts

known species, with about fifteen different plants available when cultivars are taken into account. There are also a mere ten known *Ipheion* species, so fitting these in wouldn't be too difficult either.

Some bulbs have a fairly short life when grown in temperate gardens, and this is another factor that might deter the collector. These are the species that come from areas of the world where the climate is significantly different from the average temperate garden—the Mediterranean, for example, or the Near East, or the harsh and stony steppes of Central Asia. In fact we should be rather grateful if a tulip from the deserts of Turkestan will oblige us by growing in the mild, moist Pacific North West, or in misty northern Europe, and not be surprised if the bulbs don't last for ever. But the result of this tendency to fade quietly away is that anyone who leaves their tulips (and some other genera) in the ground will be faced with the ongoing labour and expense of re-stocking part of their collection every year.

425 species and 3,200 cultivars. Numbers like these are a challenge for an individual to handle, and need serious commitment in a garden owned by an institution or a society. Other genera are also intimidatingly populous, running into the hundreds in *Tulipa*, *Lilium*, *Crocus*, *Galanthus*, *Allium*, *Fritillaria*, and *Alstroemeria*. Obviously, each represents a journey into space. However, the genus *Leucojum* has only ten

This climatic difference can have another effect. Gardeners who can't resist the temptation to increase their collection may decide to include species that are not reliable out of doors. The genus *Cyclamen* is a good example: a handful of species, such as *C. hederifolium*, are hardy, but many more, including *C. balearicum* and *C. graecum*, require frost-free conditions. The collection is then liable to end up as an exercise in greenhouse gardening, which may not be what was originally intended. Alternatively, many unusual bulbs benefit from a sun frame, which helps to give them the summer baking they would be used to if they were back home in their semi-desert habitat.

BULBS IN THE BORDER

The bulbs that can be grown in the border are mainly the smaller ones. The main thing is to prevent the emerging leaves of nearby perennials from swamping the leaves of the bulbs. The leaves must get enough sunlight to feed the bulb, otherwise the next year's flowering will suffer. Of the larger plants, the genera that are happiest in the border are the bulbous or cormous perennials, such as *Alstroemeria*, *Amaryllis*, *Arisaema*, *Arum*, *Asphodeline*, *Asphodelus*, *Crinum*, *Crocosmia*, *Galtonia*, *Schizostylis*, *Zantedeschia*, and *Zigadenus*, along with *Nectaroscordum*, the slightly tender *Chasmanthe aethiopica*, and some *Anemone*, *Allium*, and *Iris* species. To a greater or lesser extent these are all reasonably good mixers, many behaving much like a herbaceous perennial. The problem with many is that they have a longer period of dormancy than is normal for a perennial, and one needs to consider how to deal with the resultant undesirable gap. Some alstroemerias, for example, form large clumps, yet have withered away by the end of July—and so, in the words of Plato's ghost, what then?

The answer is to find a compatible companion that will guard the space until the bulb reappears once more. For example, if you plant arisaemas with the low-growing fern *Adiantum venustum*, the fern will keep the ground covered so that no gap is visible in spring, but will part to allow the stems and leaves of the arisaema to come through in midsummer. I grow the dwarf *Anemone blanda* in as many places as possible, but one plant with which it works particularly well is the silvery-leaved *Alchemilla conjuncta*, which comes fairly late into leaf, allowing the anemone to flower undisturbed first. If *Alchemilla conjuncta* forms too dense a mat for your liking, then there are many other looser-growing

ground covers one could use. In an alpine environment one could use antennarias, such as *A. dioica* 'Nyewoods Variety'.

Chionodoxas look effective planted in a carpet of ajugas, for example, the blue flowers blending well with the dark-leaved *Ajuga reptans* 'Purple Brocade'. Alternatively they can be used to underplant peonies, since the chionodoxas will have finished before the peony starts to create any shade, and the emerging peony foliage creates an attractive combination. Browny-green *Fritillaria messanensis* can be grown through a carpet of *Sedum spathulifolium* 'Purpureum', while *Hyacinthoides hispanica* can rise through tufts of *Carex testacea*, so that the grassy leaves are slightly disguised by the grassy stems of the sedge. Alstroemerias can have summer bedding plants inserted among them, such as dahlias, cosmos, or nicotianas, to conceal the gap they leave behind.

Colchicums, which come late in the season, would look good in among one of the carpeting plants mentioned in Chapter 10 (see pages 120–3), such as *Lamium galeobdolon* 'Silberteppich'.

Discovering plant combinations such as these is a matter of trial and error. Devotees of plant associations usually pass on advice about what looks good when two plants are performing simultaneously. Finding out what works in sequence is not so easy. Would the evergreen leaves of *Euphorbia myrsinites* make a good base for *Allium karataviense*? Would the late *Allium tuberosum* work well with a dicentra, such as 'Pearl Drops', the allium filling in as the dicentra begins to fade away? The only way is to try it and find out.

The most difficult bulbs to grow in a mixed border are *Narcissus*. The tall hybrids leave their foliage dying unpleasantly behind them, and the emerging

BELOW If you want to plant daffodils among perennials in the border it's best to choose dwarf cultivars, such as *Narcissus* 'Jumblie', so that the leaves won't look too unsightly later on.

leaves of adjoining perennials are likely to swamp the daffodil leaves, making it likely that the bulbs won't do so well next year. If you must plant daffodils in the border, the best to choose are the dwarf hybrids, such as 'Hawera', 'Jumblie', 'Petrel', or 'Sun Disc', which are fairly small plants—only about eight inches (20 cm) high—and therefore have less intrusive leaves. Even so the foliage could be disguised by planting the daffodils next to small grasses or sedges, or beside perennials with grass-like foliage, such as *Kniphofia* 'Little Maid' or 'Bressingham Comet', or Pacific Coast (Californian hybrid) irises, whose foliage some might argue looks a mess anyway. It is better not to dot the daffodils around but to plant them in clumps fairly tightly together, so

that they take up the equivalent amount of space as a small perennial. Alternatively the clumps can be set further back in the border, to underplant later flowers, particularly perennials that are slow into leaf such as hostas, or between deciduous ferns such as *Dryopteris*, since these plants are less likely to swamp the leaves of the narcissus. However, labelling can be a problem: it's easy to forget that the bulbs are there, but on the other hand not everyone likes a border littered with little white labels.

Tulips in the border are similarly problematic. They look good, but are even more vulnerable to being shaded out of existence than narcissus. I remember well planting a drift of the attractive tulip 'Apricot Beauty' in my own garden. They flowered happily once—and were never seen again. Nearby geranium foliage, too much, too soon, was probably to blame. If tulips are grown through ground cover, it needs to be no more than an inch or two (2.5 or 5 cm) high, and not too dense. Even then, the dying leaves of tulips won't look good flopping onto an acaena, for example, so the companion needs to be chosen with care.

As with narcissus, if tulips are in the border, it's better to grow them in places where the leaves of perennials will come quite a lot later. In between eryngiums is a suitable place, since the eryngiums, which are also sun-lovers, do not branch out and create shade too soon. And again, like narcissus, it's better to cluster tulips tightly together rather than dot them about.

Tulips come in many different categories, but the ones most likely to come up reliably year after year are the Darwin Hybrids. These are tough, and

BELOW For those of you who leave their tulip bulbs in the ground from one year to the next, among the most reliable are the Darwin Hybrid tulips, such as 'Beauty of Apeldoorn'.

BOTTOM Drifts of tulips growing in the border at Holehird Gardens, near Windermere, Cumbria. No doubt these will be lifted after flowering and replanted in the autumn.

include the bright and cheerful 'Apeldoorn', 'Apeldoorn's Elite', 'Beauty of Apeldoorn', and 'Golden Apeldoorn', and the more subtly coloured 'Burning Heart' (white with a pink flare) and 'Ivory Floradale' (pale creamy yellow). The Fosteriana and Kaufmanniana tulips are also likely to be quite persistent, though not everyone likes the dumpy habit of the Kaufmannianas. Later come the Viridiflora and Greigii types, and if these are less likely to survive it is simply because the competition is greater: the earlier a tulip flowers, the less trouble it has from the encroaching leaves of nearby perennials.

Species tulips can also be quite reliable performers, given appropriate soil conditions and no competition for sunlight. Of the ones I have tried, *Tulipa*

turkestanica is the most permanent, though this is hardly a typical tulip, with its pale colour and willowy habit. *Tulipa clusiana* and its near hybrids perform quite well, as do the attractive members of the *T. linifolia* Batalinii Group. There are so many species tulips worth a try.

Some bulbs belong to the shady border, or if your garden is on a larger scale, the woodland garden. These include snowdrops (*Galanthus*), narcissus, cyclamen, winter aconites (*Eranthis hyemalis*), bluebells (*Hyacinthoides*), and some lilies, along with some others in the "ambiguous" category of behaving more like perennials—arums, arisaemas, leucojums, and erythroniums. Many of these won't like the total shade created by buildings or evergreen trees and shrubs, although my cyclamen are happy enough.

Most prefer deciduous woodland, where the sun filters through and the trees don't come into leaf until several weeks after the bulbs have come and gone. In this situation, where there is the space available, the planting of bulbs can be in generous drifts, and take on a looser and less formal style.

BULBS, LAWNS, MEADOWS, AND NATURALIZING

A generous amount of space is needed for planting bulbs in grass. Meadows are not a good idea in a small suburban garden, not because you can't put bulbs into a suburban lawn: you can, and I've tried it. It's because the uncut grass, accompanied by flopping and dying bulb foliage, looks ragged and unkempt for many weeks at a time. Near the house, the effect is as if the gardener has gone on strike, and it makes all the parts of garden near the shaggy lawn seem neglected as well.

If you do want to try a few bulbs in a small lawn, it's best to keep to the earlier ones, so that your "experiment", as you will come to call it, will not drift on for too long. Don't have some early tulips, some mid-season tulips, and some late ones, hoping for continuity of interest, because the flowers of the later bulbs will then have to associate with the tacky foliage of the earlier ones. In a large meadow it does not matter: one can paint in broad brush-strokes. But the smaller the plot the more closely it will be scrutinized, and basically this semi-wild kind of effect looks out of place in town or suburb.

Given the space, however, the ideal solution for many bulbs is best described as the "poor meadow". This is a situation where the soil is not too fertile, the

grass doesn't grow too lush, and rank weeds are not likely to be a nuisance. The problem with an inherited agricultural field is that the farmer will have been trying to maximize its fertility for a good number of years, spreading muck or chemicals to make growth as rich as possible. Similarly, if you are converting an established garden lawn into a meadow, the lawn has probably been dosed with lawn feed for a good few years as well. Much pasture or grazing land is quite fertile in any case, and it's worth remembering that in most areas that have a temperate climate the natural habitat is not grassland at all, but forest. Do nothing to your patch of ground, and in a few years time you won't have a meadow, you'll have a wood. Unless you live on a savannah, in prairie country, or on the steppes of Mongolia, meadows are a habitat that are made in partnership with man, dependent on mowing or on the grazing of animals.

Many of the best seemingly "natural" meadows are on thin soil on underlying chalk or limestone, places where the rankest weeds such as docks and nettles can't take hold the moment your back is turned. The sub-alpine hay meadows of Switzerland are the kind of habitat to try to emulate. Drastic action may be needed at the start of this exercise, and it may be best for the existing grass in a newly acquired meadow to be killed off, since it will have been selected to maximize growth. A finer and shorter grass can be sown instead, less threatening to bulbs and more wildflower-friendly. Once the new grass is established it is important to set up a mowing regime and stick to it year on year. To get the longest succession of flowers the grass should not be cut until the start of late summer, and it will also need a cut very late in the year, so that the grass is low and neat in the spring for the shorter, early bulbs.

Bulbs will form only part of a floral meadow: a whole range of other spring flowers should accompany them, from cowslips to clover, buttercups to moon daisies, blue *Geranium pratense*, orchids, and a whole range of interesting umbellifers, and these can all be sown at the same time as the new grass species. Other plants of particular interest can be added later by spot planting, if desired. It's worth finding out what is native, or at least will look native, in your area and what will flourish for you without becoming aggressive. Meadow gardening is part science and part serendipity—that is part of the pleasure. Your location will help you decide whether you are going to stick to the native look, which can

BELOW Some larger liliaceous plants can be grown either in grass or in the border, such as *Asphodeline lutea*, or yellow asphodel, reaching a height of three feet (90 cm), from the Mediterranean area.

OPPOSITE Naturalized daffodils at Dyffryn Gardens, near Cardiff. This is the best way to grow daffodils, as nature intended, but of course not many people have this amount of space.

be a little restrictive (in England, for example, it would basically mean daffodils), or whether you could add a dash of the exotic with scarlet tulips or anything else colourful that will grow well for you.

Among early bulbs that do well grown in short grass are snowdrops, *Scilla bifolia*, triteleias, and crocuses. *Crocus vernus* and *C. tommasinianus* are both suitable, and the "tommies" will multiply very rewardingly: the darker forms are especially good. It's best not to mix plants of the same height, but to have separate drifts of separate kinds. If you do want a mixture, have a tall bulb that flowers simultaneously with a short bulb of a contrasting colour.

Later on in the season come *Narcissus*, such as the hoop-petticoat daffodil *N. bulbocodium* as well as *N. pseudonarcissus* (a British native), along with fritillaries such as *Fritillaria meleagris* and the brownish-green *F. pyrenaica*, blue grape hyacinths (*Muscari*), and a fabulous range of species (or hybrid)

tulips, in brilliant reds and oranges that look particularly stunning in grass. Later still come the white-coloured "pheasant's eye" *Narcissus poeticus*, white ornithogalums, and deep blue *Iris latifolia*, and taller-growing bulbs such as the summer snowflake (*Leucojum aestivum*), blue *Camassia quamash* (previously *C. esculenta*), *Asphodelus*, *Asphodeline*, *Anthericum*, *Lilium martagon*, in reds, pinks, or even white; yellow *Lilium pyrenaicum*, and magenta *Gladiolus communis* subsp. *byzantinus*. Some of these you may have to mow round, rather than mow over. For autumn, colchicums are also happy in grass, and the autumn cutting regime will have to take account of these. If a deciduous tree stands in your meadow area, then beneath it is the place to plant snowdrops, winter aconites, and erythroniums; if the grass there is really thin, carpets of cyclamen are easy to create, as they seed themselves where they are happy. Just lift a few after they have flowered and spread them around a bit.

Of course, the meadow is no place for rarities. No one wants to spend time and effort raising a rare plant from seed and then drop it into a meadow, like a needle in a haystack. It may be very happy there, but it may not, and in any case, will you ever be able to find it again? Cost is another obvious factor: to slip an expensive plant into the mêlée of a meadow seems far too risky a strategy. The collector of rare or expensive species needs to build up the comfort of numbers before he or she can afford to try treasured plants in a meadow.

The way to plant in grass is in irregular drifts and scatterings, and if it's *Narcissus*, to plant by the thousand, or at least by the hundred. It's advisable to

put several bulbs in one hole, so that you get reasonable clumps to start off with. In nature, one sees what looks like a million of one kind of narcissus, accompanied by a million of some other wild thing. In other words, there is generally only one species each of a genus of plants—in a Pyrenean meadow, for example, there will generally only be one *Narcissus* species, one *Anemone* species, and so on. Of course there may be "that odd white one", but this is unusual. The message of this observation is that if, for example, we are planting narcissus in a meadow, all the flowers that can be taken in with one glance should be of the same species. Mixed species or mixed hybrids will look a muddle, and unnatural.

So while planting in grass would seem to be an obvious option for a serious collection of hybrid *Narcissus*, in practice, small clusters of fifty (or five hundred) different kinds in a field would look fairly awful, and not the least bit like any respectable meadow. So some man-made, or more horticultural, setting seems preferable. An orchard, which has rough grass, but also has rows of old fruit trees, would seem ideal. The narcissus are tough, and won't get lost. The trees have probably already established some kind of geometry, having been planted in rows, so blocks of narcissus in between will not look too much out of place.

THE GRAVEL GARDEN

More delicate bulbs prefer not to have to do battle with grass, and instead will do well in a gravel garden. The advantage of gravel is that it is usually acceptable as a surface to look at, whereas a patch of bare earth looks as though it is a gap waiting to be filled. In this way gravel takes away the pressure to double-plant the place where you have the bulbs—useful for the more delicate species that don't really appreciate competition or even companionship.

BELOW Many small
bulbs are very happy in the
warmth and free-draining
environment of the gravel
bed. This one is *Chionodoxa
luciliae* 'Gigantea'.

Gravel also absorbs heat in summer, and creates a well-drained top layer where there can be no risk of water collecting on the surface—all beneficial to bulbs. It is easier to pull weeds out of gravel than from ordinary soil, and there is even the bonus that white labels show up less against pale gravel than they do in brown soil. As long as the bed is in full sun this will create conditions that will be enjoyed by many Mediterranean-type plants—not just bulbs. If a mixed border is planned, then the bulbs can be planted along the front, associated with low-growing companions, while at the back of the border a range of perennials, shrubs, and shrublets hailing from the *maquis* habitat will give the bulbs an appropriate setting along with additional shelter and warmth.

Almost all types of bulb are suitable for planting in gravel, although one would no doubt want to exclude those known to be woodlanders. Tulips are particularly happy there. Anemones, foxtail lilies (*Eremurus*), fritillarias, bulbous irises, grape hyacinths (*Muscari*), nerines, *Ranunculus*, schizostylis, sternbergias, and tulbaghias are all suitable bulbs for the well-drained gravel bed, as are the more delicate Mediterranean *Narcissus* species, the less vigorous crocuses, and non-seeding (non-pestiferous) alliums. In milder districts these conditions would also be ideal for the highly desirable but slightly tender genera such as × *Amarcrinum*, *Belamcanda*, *Rhodophiala*,

drastic) plan might be to remove six inches (15 cm) of topsoil, add six inches (15cm) of sharp, coarse gravel, put the topsoil back, and then top-dress with a suitable gravel that is pleasing to the eye. This also has the effect of raising the bed slightly, further improving its drainage. It is important, however, to make sure that this well-drained bed drains away somewhere, otherwise it will act in quite the reverse manner and your well-drained bed will actually be a pit that collects water, especially if the subsoil contains any clay.

A gravel bed also makes it possible to eliminate the conventional (and sometimes boring) arrangement of a hard and rigid line between border and path. The adjoining path can be made of the same gravel being used in the border, so that path and border then blend. But you do have to hope that visitors show some sense and don't walk on the labels marking the spot at the edge of the border proper, where your little sternbergias (or whatever else you've planted) are going to come up.

RAISED BEDS

The next stage in terms of creating special conditions for a bulb collection is to lift the level of the bed above the surrounding ground, and create a raised bed with retaining walls. This may solve drainage problems, but may create visual problems in the garden instead. A raised bed draws attention to itself, and doesn't suit every garden situation, particularly if the plants it contains are small. A raised bed with three feet (90 cm) high shrubs in it is one thing, but a raised bed full of chionodoxas or crocuses can look out of proportion: the plants will look like whiskers

Tigridia, *Watsonia*, and *Zephyranthes*, although some of these generate quite a lot of foliage.

If the bed is for a collection of bulbs of one particular type or genus, then the specification of the soil and subsoil can be purpose-made to suit the plants. Beneath the gravel one can carry out any special preparations that will suit the plants in question. To improve a heavy soil, for example, a typical (if

BELOW Sternbergias growing in gravel at the Sir Harold Hillier Gardens, near Winchester, Hampshire.

OPPOSITE Slightly tender bulbous plants, such as tigridias, benefit from the warmth and well-drained conditions provided by gravel. Tigridias come in various colours, but always with extraordinary markings to the central cup.

on a pig's back. Even limiting the small plants to the front edges of the bed doesn't resolve things entirely. The front edge will look much better if the plants in it are of the size and habit of iberis, *Euphorbia myrsinites*, or *Persicaria affinis*, which will scramble nicely over the wall and soften the hard edge. One can tuck in a few bulbs here and there in this regime, but if bulbs are to form a high proportion of the planting, a border dressed with gravel is probably a better solution in terms of the appearance of the garden. But such beds could always be placed out of sight, in the "working" part of the garden.

However, raised beds can be ornamental and form part of the main garden, but several factors have to be borne in mind. To begin with, their position within the garden needs to be carefully thought about. Sometimes one sees raised beds placed in quite random positions, floating at odd angles in a sea of grass. It's far better if the lines and shapes of the beds relate to the overall garden scheme—in other words, the geometry of the beds needs to be part of the geometry of the garden. If there are walls in the garden, then it seems reasonable for the lines of the dwarf walls to have some rational relationship with the lines of the higher walls. On the other hand, some form of relief from long straight lines may also be needed, to prevent the dwarf walls looking too mechanical and utilitarian. In addition the materials that the beds are made of need to be attractive to look at—stone, good-quality brick, or even timber sleepers (anything except concrete blocks).

The height of such beds also needs thought. Some books recommend that raised beds should be about the height of a dining-room table, to prevent you

getting a stiff back as you bend over them. Unfortunately the higher the beds are, the more intrusive and harsh they will look. Ideally, any raised bed more than fifteen inches (40 cm) in height ought to have another bed in front of it, which will allow some greenery to be planted in front of the wall to create a softening effect against the intrusive vertical surface. The net result of this is to make access to the bed impractical. So a balance has to be struck, and considering one will not be working at these beds all the time, a lower height for the bed seems preferable.

PAMPERING YOUR DARLINGS

The next stage in dedication is to go for raised beds constructed in such a way that glass frames can be put over them. This will give protection in winter

and additional heat in summer, giving many unusual bulbs the summer baking they would be used to if they were back home. In this case the beds obviously have to be regular in shape, so that the frames can be placed over them sensibly and safely. The glass will have to be set at a slight slope—to allow the rainwater to run off them—and a way also has to be devised to remove and store the frames when they are not required.

The effect, unfortunately, won't look much like a border, but more as if you were gardening in boxes, which is not a particularly attractive notion. The books may tell you that such beds "can easily be built from breeze blocks", but wait a moment—surely this will be like keeping your plants in the horticultural equivalent of a bus shelter? In my view, a

beautiful plant deserves an attractive setting. If the plant is all, and the setting irrelevant, well, that's fine. But in that case such beds definitely need to be tucked away in a corner of the garden along with the potting-up area and the compost heap.

The advantage of such elaborate beds is that everything the plant requires in the way of protection, or other particular needs, can be provided. The down side is that such an alien environment will overpower the plant in question. Its beauty will be like that of one fish in a goldfish bowl again, rather than the more realistic effect created when the fish lives in the setting of a large, planted aquarium.

Beyond this, we reach greenhouses, plastic tunnels, and alpine houses—but these are not within the scope of this book.

13
Alpines

ALPINES ARE SMALL PLANTS by nature, and we admire them for their miniature beauty and the amazing detail of their flowers. There's no point growing them for the contribution they make to the garden picture as a whole, however, as they simply aren't big enough to be effective at that scale. No matter how attractive alpines are in themselves, in garden-making terms they are decoration on the cake. Even if you were to plant a large area with one type of alpine you still wouldn't have a big plant, although you might have a good patch of ground cover. Stand back to take a general photograph of the garden, and whether that scrap of blue is a *Veronica*, a *Campanula*, or a *Lithodora* won't make much difference. Closer to, the picture changes as we move into a new mode of seeing.

THE LAND OF LILLIPUT

If one of our aims is to make a pleasing garden picture, plants the size of alpines have to be used in among other, larger plants, but this may not suit the more specialized plants from montane habitats. Although many of these small plants demand a certain amount of care, their most basic need is for *Lebensraum*, space of their own, where other plants won't crowd in on them or swamp them. We should not let the fact that they are diminutive tempt us to "squeeze them in" somewhere where there are a few spare inches. They need to go in places where they will look comfortable.

The term "Alpine" is a broad one which has come to mean small plants of any description, and while some of them do need special conditions, others are much more flexible, and it shouldn't be difficult

OPPOSITE *Campanula* growing in the Italian alps, not far from Mont Blanc. Scree looks fine when there are huge mountains all around, but in gardens it's not quite so appealing.

BELOW Most alpines prefer to grow in a sunny open position, but some, such as *Saxifraga* 'Gregor Mendel' (syn. *S.* × *apiculata*), are shade tolerant.

to find places for the easier-going ones somewhere in the garden. Helianthemums, aubrietas, pinks, *Artemisia schmidtiana* 'Nana', *Asarum europaeum*, *Bergenia* 'Wintermärchen', *Geranium dalmaticum*, *G. sanguineum* var. *striatum*, *Sedum cauticola*, *Tanacetum haradjani* as well as many others can all cope with life at the front of the mixed border, especially where there is paving or gravel rather than grass to contend with.

But if the plants in question have specific needs, such as perfect drainage, then the number of corners that they can be tucked into will be limited, or even non-existent. As a general rule alpines do prefer well-drained soil, although many of them simultaneously need some moisture-retentive organic matter as well. They also need plenty of light—which is not surprising, considering that these are plants that typically grow on the tops of mountains. Some of them will be happy to face north—many a mountainside faces north—but light must still reach them: the type of perma-shade created by buildings or tall trees won't do. Some prefer protection from the full heat of the sun, such as the saxifrages in the Porphyrion group, which includes *Saxifraga burseriana*, *S.* 'Gregor Mendel' (syn. *S.* × *apiculata*), and *S. federici-augusti* subsp. *grisebachii*. Many other alpines hate winter wet, especially the true alpines that are accustomed to the free-draining screes and gritty soil of mountain slopes, so this limits where they can be placed in the garden.

When considering some of the more "difficult" alpine species it may be worth considering whether the presentation of the collection should be ornamental at all. Do we insist on the plants looking

good grouped or associated with others, or are we content simply to grow them in a situation that suits them, where they can be studied one by one, in detail? If order and the ability to compare and contrast are all that matter, it may be better to treat a one-genus alpine collection as a separate exercise from making a garden. The systematic way to approach this would be to grow the plants in neat rows, labelling them neatly. But a long row of small plants will look exactly what it is—a long row of small plants—and although each specimen may be

and this will obviously look more attractive than eighteen campanulas in a row. But elsewhere there would be an orderly display that doesn't pretend to be attractive as a visual arrangement.

TROUGHS

A common way to grow tiny plants that encourages the onlooker to get into "close focus" mode is to plant alpines in troughs. Good drainage is easily provided, though watering may also be required in summer. This is gardening in miniature, where small-scale plant associations can be made and the results have charm of their own. Obviously this approach has its limitations: even in a large garden one cannot have endless numbers of troughs and sinks, or the effect becomes uncomfortably cluttered. More than, say, about twenty terracotta bowls containing different sempervivums tends to start looking obsessive rather than decorative.

Again, some alpines can be made to grow on a lump of tufa. But there are only so many lumps of tufa one can have about the place. If a large collection of alpines is involved, troughs, sinks, bowls, and chunks of tufa can only be expected to house a small proportion of the total numbers. I put my own troughs and sinks into the border, as they look better nestling against a dwarf shrub or two, rather than sitting starkly on paving slabs.

THE ROCK GARDEN

Some people classify alpines as rock plants, but this presupposes the existence of something called a rock garden, which not everyone possesses, or even wants. Unfortunately a rock garden within a town garden

interesting close to, the arrangement as a whole will inevitably have that vegetable-plot look.

The ideal arrangement is to have "Both-And", as we saw previously with perennials. In this scenario the plants are grown ornamentally in the garden: three campanulas here beside a dwarf artemisia, one there beside a tanacetum, two more somewhere else,

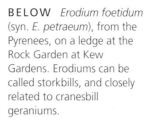

or in suburbia often looks incongruous. The chances that your garden just happens to be full of massive rocks are remote, unless of course you live in a quarry, or on the side of the Rocky Mountains. The concept "rockery" is fine in principle, but what puts many people off them is that rockeries as seen in suburban gardens are frequently a disaster. Very commonly they appear to consist of a lorryload of rocks about twelve inches long and nine inches wide (30 and 20 cm) that have been thoughtlessly dumped on a mound of soil.

For any chance of success with a rockery you need space, and you also need a reasonable budget. The larger the scale the more likely it is that the result will be successful, and the rocks need to be big. The rule of thumb is that unless you need a crane to lift them then the rocks are too small. They also look best when sympathetic in colour and geology to the rocks that occur naturally in the area, and they must all be of the same type. At Kew Gardens the (very

large) rock garden is sunk deep into the ground, and the rocks look as if they had been there all the time, lurking under the surface.

If there is a slight fall to the garden, so much the better. At least the disastrous "mound" effect can be avoided, the so-called dog's grave, as Reginald Farrer called it. A slope enables you to make an effective rock garden by using rocks to form a series of steps running along the contours, creating flattish areas for plants in between. The rocks can be laid out either in a roughly straight line or, better still, a gently curving serpentine line, with the rocks forming the front face of the step. The top surface of adjoining rocks should be roughly continuous, and behind the rocks level gravel beds can be created, with the plants sitting comfortably on the ledge, or step. In the vertical gaps between the rocks, one can plant *Ramonda myconi*, or *Haberlea rhodopensis* perhaps. Try to avoid the temptation to create that mini-waterfall with water appearing from nowhere

RIGHT An attractive fritillary, *Fritillaria pyrenaica*, let down by its setting—a bleak expanse of gravel.

and cascading down into a mini-pool. However, this is fine for gardens that also feature gnomes, giant toadstools, and mini-windmills.

Within the garden, the setting or context of the rock garden needs to be considered. A rock garden is pretending to be a certain kind of alpine habitat, and the greater the verisimilitude the better it will look. This is why the background needs particular care, because in the world of our imagination the top of the rock garden is the equivalent of the mountain-top. Somehow we need to bridge the change in scale between the miniature alpine world and the real world beyond. A rock garden with a garden shed behind it looks particularly farcical, and the same goes for a greenhouse or even a bare fence. A greenhouse on a mountaintop? Smallish shrubs planted behind or even at the top of the rock garden will help to create a reasonably realistic backdrop or break between the small rock garden and its wider surroundings. *Sorbus reducta*, *Salix helvetica*, *Ballota pseudodictamnus*, *Coprosma* species, and a range of small hebes could all be tried. At Kew, the rock garden sits in a rectangular area bordered on one side by a high brick wall, which divides the rock garden from the Order Beds. Unfortunately there are places where the wall intrudes, and this destroys the illusion, saying "garden" when we should be thinking "mountain".

GRAVEL, RAISED BEDS, AND TAPESTRY GARDENS

A gravel garden such as the one discussed in the chapter on bulbs is also likely to give alpines the conditions they like, but it may not look ideal in this case. This is simply because all the plants are small, and the effect of a large gravel surface littered with little blobs or stalks may not be very pleasing. For a gravel garden to provide a home for alpines it works better if it is a mixed border, such the Mediterranean border discussed earlier (see page 146). In this scenario, the back of the border can have larger plants, giving variation in height and scale, and then the onlooker doesn't feel so much like an uncomfortable Gulliver among the Lilliputians. The same applies to a scree garden, although on the whole an artificial scree garden is more difficult to handle than a gravel garden. Has a lorry accidentally dropped its load of

BELOW Scree may be the correct habitat for some plants, but doesn't look very pretty in the garden.

BOTTOM Raised beds have the dual advantages of bringing tiny plants nearer the eye, and making access slightly easier. If the copings are broad enough and are at the right height—about sixteen inches (40 cm)— they could even provide somewhere to sit.

scalpings on its way to some road-building scheme? One hopes not. If you want to grow a plant that demands a scree bed, such as *Calandrinia umbellata*, it's preferable to create a little local area of scree for it within the gravel or rock garden.

Another strategy to consider is to plant alpines in raised beds. Unlike the rock garden situation, there is no need to pretend that the side of Mont Blanc has suddenly manifested itself in your own backyard. With raised beds, one accepts that the plants have a man-made setting. But as we noted in Chapter 12 (see pages 147–9), some larger plants will be needed if the scale is to look right.

BELOW AND BOTTOM
Acaena affinis (below) and
Phlox subulata 'McDaniel's
Cushion' (bottom). Both
of these are tiny plants,
suitable candidates for
the "tapestry garden".

An alternative planting idea for alpines is the "tapestry garden", which is sometimes called an alpine pavement. I confess I've never seen this carried through to completion, but I did design one once. Sadly it was never carried out, for various reasons which have a long and tedious history. The idea of the tapestry garden is to give the general impression of a formal Persian carpet. You begin with a rectangular paved area, laid out with more than half the paving slabs omitted and gravel put down to fill in the gaps, but leaving a continuous

border of slabs round the edge, where you can conveniently walk. The gaps between the slabs are planted as mini gravel gardens, where alpines can find homes and spill out on to the surrounding paving stones.

In the tapestry garden I was planning, the flowers were all to conform to a strict colour scheme—dark red, purple, khaki, apricots, and browns—all the rich colours of an oriental carpet. My tapestry garden was also to be patterned: the gaps in the slabs were not just random, but created a geometrical arrangement, again echoing the oriental carpet theme. But plants being what they are, there would be a happy blend of formality and informality. Plants suitable for such a tapestry garden might include such examples as acaenas, *Antennaria rosea*, *Cerastium tomentosum* var. *columnae*, *Leptinella* (previously *Cotula*) *squalida*, cyclamen, dianthus, *Frankenia thymifolia*, *Geranium dalmaticum*, helianthemums, iberis, *Phlox subulata*, *Sagina subulata* var. *glabrata* 'Aurea', sedums, and thymes.

ALPINE ASSOCIATIONS

Planting within a rock garden, or on a raised bed, presents few other difficulties from a design point of view. Firstly a certain number of evergreen plants will be needed if the beds are to look at all attractive in winter. Some thought could also be given to the kind of habitat being created, and whether the plants being planted together could be imagined as belonging to similar habitats. Otherwise the planting plan can follow the same kind of ideas as govern other groups of plants—some variety is needed, and some consistency. Consistency of scale in particular

needs to be considered. Some books on alpines include plants such as trilliums, but to my mind these belong with perennials. They tend to look like giants if planted among average alpines.

Some height and verticality might be needed, to contrast with mat-forming alpines, and this can be obtained from plants such as *Euphorbia rigida*, *Acorus gramineus* 'Hakuro-nishiki', dwarf grasses, or an exceedingly dwarf phormium I grow, about six inches (15 cm) tall, whose name I haven't yet discovered. A few stars of the show will also benefit the display; what is needed are strong-charactered plants on a small scale, such as *Celmisia coriacea*, the alpine thistle *Carlina acaulis*, *Hebe lycopodioides*, or one or two dwarf conifers.

PART

3

Plant Associations,
Beds, and Borders

14
Plant associations

So far we have looked at the general issues that arise when we try to combine the ambition to collect interesting plants with the aim of making an attractive garden. We have considered the various kinds of plant material that go to make a garden—trees, shrubs, and so on—and explored the pleasures and problems that each present. However, few of us want to grow plants in isolation (like one goldfish in a bowl), or lined out in rows, and therefore something remains to said about putting plants together, commonly called the art of plant association.

TIMES AND CONDITIONS
Before we explore ideas about colour, contrast, foliage, or the relationship of one plant shape to the next, two basic observations should be made about placing plants together. First of all, the two plants must either flower at the same time, or at least be ornamental simultaneously. This may sound obvious, but when one is indoors in the middle of winter, thinking of ways to improve the garden, it can be surprisingly easy to forget exactly when a particular plant is at its best. It's no good, for example, imagining that the flowers of *Euphorbia griffithii* would look good with *Kniphofia* 'Tawny King', because the euphorbia display will be over before the kniphofia has started. However, this is not an exact science, because in many parts of the world the pattern of climate and seasons varies from year to year: extra rain will bring those plants forward that like a bit more moisture, while a cold snap will hold others back.

The second principle to be observed when putting plants together is that the two plants in question must like the same conditions. A plant from a hot, dry desert will never be happy next to a bog plant. The leaves may contrast very nicely and the flowers might blend, but if they can't live together it's not going to work. In some cases the nature of the area to be planted will impose obvious limitations. An area of shady woodland or a dry and sunny gravel garden are situations where the soil and microclimate will

PREVIOUS PAGES
A large and complex colour
scheme at Bressingham
Gardens, with pale blue
agapanthus, crocosmias,
eryngiums, Shasta daisies,
Eupatorium and variegated
Miscanthus.

BELOW An achillea
growing with *Knautia
macedonica*. Rather than
having two plants side
by side, a more original
way of putting two plants
together is to allow them
to intermingle.

BELOW Plants growing
next to each other have to
share the same preferences
for soil conditions, light and
shade, and so on. Here,
Ligularia 'The Rocket' and
Rodgersia pinnata are seen
flourishing in woodland
conditions in semi-shade.

The plants chosen also need to look as though they belong together, or appear as if they came from roughly the same habitat. In our minds we associate certain plants with particular situations. For example, plants with fleshy, succulent leaves have developed them as a way of storing moisture in a hot and dry climate, and knowing this fact has an effect on the types of plants we expect to see associated with them. For instance, in terms of colour, *Sedum telephium* 'Matrona' would blend nicely with *Calluna vulgaris* 'Golden Feather', and technically they could be grown together in an average soil. But that would not stop them looking incongruous, because we know quite well in our minds that (on the whole) the larger sedums like Mediterranean conditions, while heathers belong to cool, damp moorland.

demand to be taken into account. But in average conditions, mistakes are easier to make. Pulmonarias flower at about the same time as several good euphorbias, for example, but this will be no use to us, since most euphorbias want sun and good drainage, while pulmonarias prefer shade and woodland soil, otherwise they scorch and look terrible.

There are other methods of dividing plants into categories—wild versus cultivated, for example, or

BELOW The delicate rose 'Queen Mother' looks uncomfortable here in the shadow of the bold but coarse *Senecio doria*. The combination of orange and pale pink is also fairly dire.

persicarias, and *Geranium pratense*. The colours didn't match, either—one so pale and delicate, the other so bright and brash—and a third plant in the group did nothing to bridge the gap. Just to add insult to injury, it was an orange crocosmia, which looked quite horrendous next to the pale pink rose.

When building a collection it's worthwhile keeping in mind what kind of plants you are growing. If it's sedums that interest you, it's not that difficult to make a list of "sedum-y" things that will blend in with them and look right—other plants with fleshy leaves, various sun-lovers, and so on. However, some genera contain a diverse range of plant forms. *Euphorbia capitulata*, which comes from the top of the Carpathian mountains in Eastern Europe and is only one inch (2.5 cm) high, will obviously need a very different home from the average euphorbia, while *Euphorbia soongarica*, a relative giant from Central Asia up to six feet (1.8 m) tall, will also need appropriate placing.

COMPATIBILITY AND SUCCESSFUL RELATIONSHIPS

Similarity of height also needs to be borne in mind when considering plant associations—for example, it's difficult to create a relationship between a helianthus and a hosta, since it's nearly impossible to look up at the one and down at the other at the same time. There needs to be a gradation of height in a border, but if two plants are meant to be side-by-side companions, then one of them needs to be at least two-thirds the height of the other. However, "side-by-side" is not the only relationship that is possible in planting schemes.

coarse versus neat and refined. I remember seeing an unhappy grouping of plants (in an otherwise admirable garden) where the large perennial *Senecio doria*, a slightly coarse, bright yellow ragwort relative, sat next to the delicate pale pink patio rose 'Queen Mother'. Both are good plants, but one belongs in the wild garden, the other near to the house. The rose needed a rose garden, or a mixed border with choice perennials, while the senecio should have been with tougher plants, in a semi-wild border, perhaps, with umbellifers, ornamental grasses,

Sometimes side-by-side looks too competitive, especially if both plants are strong characters. In design terms, the word used is "duality", which describes a situation in which the viewer isn't able to decide which of two rival objects is dominant. This is why some shrub associations fail. A general background of shrubs with slightly varying characters is fine, but if one is brightly variegated, the next is an arching, prickly berberis, and the next the feature plant *Mahonia × media* 'Charity', they will all be vying for attention, and the effect will be chaotic.

An alternative to side-by-side is the "feature-and-background" relationship, in which a plant with a distinct shape or striking colour stands out in front of plain but contrasting background foliage. An example would be lemon-yellow kniphofias in front of *Berberis thunbergii* f. *atropurpurea*. The berberis provides plain, dark foliage that contrasts with the colour of the feature plant. I have also seen *Verbascum* 'Pink Domino' used in front of purple berberis, the colours in this case sympathetic rather than contrasting. Another example would be the blackish

BELOW A dwarf
phormium growing in a
carpet of *Euphorbia
cyparissias* 'Fens Ruby'. An
effective way to associate
two plants is to place a
feature plant within a low-
growing carpeter.

spikes of *Veratrum nigrum* showing up well in front of the white-variegated foliage of *Cornus alba* 'Elegantissima'. Whatever the two plants, the one in the background clearly needs to be taller and wider than the feature plant in front.

In this scenario there also needs to be a degree of contrast between two adjoining plants. Blue *Iris sibirica* in front of a low-growing blue ceanothus may flower at the same time, but blue against blue won't show up. Try finding a black button on a black carpet—it's extremely difficult. This is why successful white gardens are often set within a framework of dwarf box hedges. The dark colour of the box provides a perfect background, or base, for white flowers. When white is against white, like

sheep in a snowy field, some of the plants will be hard to see, and those that look less white than others will not be flattered.

It's also important for the background not to be distracting or to overpower the feature plant. A peach-coloured *Iris germanica* variety planted in front of a brilliantly coloured *Papaver* cultivar, for example, isn't going to show to advantage, because the brighter colour of the poppy will overshadow it. The splashes of scarlet (or whatever colour) behind the iris will compete too strongly for attention.

A similar solution is to position a feature plant within a low carpeter, creating an arrangement that in design terminology is called "articulation". A few examples have already been given in the section on ground cover (see pages 120–3). *Stipa gigantea* rising high out of a sea of a short form of *Euphorbia cyparissias* would be a typical example, or the brilliant orange heads of *Kniphofia uvaria* within a drift of low, khaki-green *Carex testacea*. On a much larger scale one could have a full-grown *Fatsia japonica* towering, umbrella-like, not over shrubs, but over a carpet of ferns, hostas, and cyclamen. Similarly a delicate-looking, variegated feature bamboo could emerge from a contrasting base provided by plants with bold foliage, such as × *Fatshedera lizei* or *Hedera hibernica*. An even larger example would be a multi-stemmed silver birch standing in a carpet of heathers, *Vaccinium*, and *Arctostaphylos*.

Another way to create interesting plant associations is to avoid similarity of overall plant shape, and find other visual links between plants. Instead of leafy perennial A next to leafy perennial B, one can be more imaginative. For instance, at Foggy Bottom,

Adrian Bloom's garden at Bressingham, Norfolk, I saw yellow and black rudbeckias (leafy perennials) grouped with an unlabelled *Kniphofia* (all spikes) with burned apricot flowers fading to white, and alongside was the soft-and-floppy, ripe corn-coloured ornamental grass, *Stipa tenuissima*. These three quite different plant forms (leafy perennial/monocot/grass) were linked by their sympathetic colours: yellow, tawny, and corn-coloured, respectively. Another inventive association consisted of three even more different plants: a white kniphofia with the red grass *Imperata cylindrica* 'Rubra', and, as if that wasn't interesting enough, they were backed by spiky dwarf blue conifers—either spruce (*Picea*) or possibly dwarf *Cedrus* cultivars. I'm no lover of

dwarf blue conifers, but in this situation they looked quite extraordinary . Here were plants put together in a way that defied all the customary and conventional categories, such as "herbaceous border" or "conifer garden".

MIXING AND MINGLING

Another alternative to the side-by-side arrangement is to steal an effect from the meadow garden and associate plants by creating an interweaving effect. For example, the maroon, scabious-like flowers of *Knautia macedonica* look good weaving in and out of a dwarf yellow achillea. In my own garden I have *Vinca major* 'Variegata' (often called 'Elegantissima') growing in among *Euphorbia robbiae*: two tough

is something one has to experiment with. *Daphne cneorum* 'Eximia', for example, tolerates the intermingling stems of the perennial candytuft *Iberis sempervirens*, but hebes don't like to be encroached upon, as dieback is likely to occur, spoiling the appearance of the plant.

Some bulbs, such as alliums, can be planted so that they grow through low perennials, again creating an intermingling effect. *Allium sphaerocephalon* looks good coming up through *Gypsophila* 'Rosen-schleier' (commonly known as "Rosy Veil"). Large purple alliums work especially well seen emerging through half-grown perennials. I like to see *Nectaroscordum siculum* subsp. *bulgaricum* (which is an interesting-looking plant, but just ignore the smell) growing among cranesbill geraniums. Some plants are scramblers as well as weavers: *Ammi majus*, for example, an annual umbellifer with a dainty, lacy effect, will weave its way vertically as well as horizontally through other plants. Shrubs or tall, tough perennials are the best companions for this plant. Some gardeners allow aquilegia seedlings to fill gaps between other plants, only weeding them out once they've flowered. I've also seen love-in-a-mist, *Nigella*, filling gaps very attractively, even in among the stems of irises—although in the long run this may not do the irises much good, as the sun needs to be able to get to the rhizomes.

There are also biennials that can be given the freedom to sow themselves around and dot themselves in among other plants, such as honesty (*Lunaria*), the innocuous and spindly *Euphorbia corallioides*, purple, tall-stemmed *Verbena bonariensis*, furry grey verbascums, and foxgloves. However,

plants in a tough place, in dry shade. *Omphalodes cappadocica* will happily mingle with ferns. Helianthemums are also quite content to scramble into suitably tough plants taller than themselves.

Many cranesbill geraniums make excellent weavers, in particular *Geranium* × *riversleaianum* 'Russell Prichard' and 'Mavis Simpson'. Some geraniums may be rather too vigorous: you have to make sure the weaver doesn't become a smotherer. Erodiums, which are related to geraniums, are also weavers, but are smaller and, therefore, less threatening. Some plants mingle, others don't, and this

while tolerance of self-sown seedlings is fine in the so-called wild garden, elsewhere it's a risky policy which can get out of hand. Leave too many geranium seedlings around, and your garden will be swamped. Don't imagine any of them is a rare and valuable new hybrid—it's a one in a million chance, not worth spoiling your garden for.

COLOUR

Colour is the feature most commonly considered when we start to put plants together. This usually means flower colour, but it could also mean foliage, or possibly a combination of the two. An example of this approach at its simplest would be to plant *Coreopsis verticillata* next to *Aster* × *frikartii* 'Mönch', the blue with the yellow, two plants compatible in height, flowering side by side. Another example could be a form of *Eupatorium* (Joe Pye weed), such as *E. purpureum* 'Purple Bush', next to *Veronicastrum virginicum* 'Album'—two tall perennials, contrasting pleasantly in flower shape and blending in colour.

Colour combinations may be a matter of personal taste but, nevertheless, some guidelines may prove helpful. In theory almost any two colours can be combined. You can put pink with orange—but only if you do it deliberately as part of a pink and orange scheme, not if it looks like carelessness. *Berberis darwinii* next to *Prunus* 'Kanzan' just looks abysmal.

There are two simple ways of tackling colour schemes. The first is to divide the pack in two. On one side you put the pinks-mauves-blues-whites-and-silvers, and on the other the creams-yellows-oranges-maroons-and-browns. Keep these two groups apart and you will be safe. For example, to give us the pinks-mauves-blues-whites-and-silvers, we could plant a border mainly of perennials: *Penstemon* 'Hidcote Pink', *Geranium* × *oxonianum* 'Wargrave Pink', and *Astrantia* 'Buckland' (silvery-pink); *Acanthus mollis* (mauve and white), *Phlox paniculata* 'Vintage Wine' (royal purple), *Erigeron* 'Schwarzes Meer' (deep mauve daisies), and *Eryngium* × *tripartitum* (prickly, metallic mauvey-blue); *Campanula lactiflora* 'Prichard's Variety' (rich blue), *Geranium* 'Rozanne' (deep blue), *Geranium* 'Johnson's Blue', *Salvia officinalis* 'Purpurascens' (mauvey-grey foliage,

LEFT The traditional solution—two leafy perennials growing side by side in a "one + one" association: the blue daisies of *Aster × frikartii* 'Mönch' and the yellow flowers of *Coreopsis verticillata*.

blue flowers), and *Elymus magellanicus* (a blue-coloured grass); *Geranium clarkei* 'Kashmir White' (white flowers with a hint of mauve), *Phlox maculata* 'Schneelawine' (pure white, often called 'Avalanche'), and *Gypsophila* 'Rosenschleier' (pale pinky-white flowers); and onopordums (silvery-white giant thistles), *Artemisia* 'Powis Castle' (silvery-grey) and *Phlomis italica* (silver foliage with occasional pink-coloured flowers).

In a separate border, the other half of the pack, the creams-yellows-oranges-maroons-and-browns, could typically contain perennials such as *Anthemis tinctoria* 'Sauce Hollandaise' (creamy-yellow daisies), *Hemerocallis* 'Annie Welch' (a cream-coloured daylily), and *Euphorbia seguieriana* subsp. *niciciana* (yellowy-green with silvery foliage); *Achillea* 'Coronation Gold' (flat yellow flowerheads), *Crocosmia × crocosmiiflora* 'Lady Hamilton' (spikes of yellow flowers), heliopsis (yellow daisies), rudbeckias (yellow with a black eye), and *Hemerocallis* 'Fashion Model' (pale apricot); *Achillea* 'Fanal' (dusky

orange), *Helenium* 'Sahin's Early Flowerer' (orange-yellow), *Kniphofia rooperi* (orange poker-spikes), low-growing orange helianthemums, *Anthemis sancti-johannis* (orange flowers), *Crocosmia* 'Severn Sunrise' (orange-red), *Euphorbia griffithii* (burned orange), and *Helenium* 'Coppelia' (coppery-orange); *Kniphofia uvaria* 'Nobilis' (scarlet), *Dahlia* 'Bishop of Llandaff' (dark red), and *Hemerocallis* 'Stafford' (red); and *Hemerocallis* 'Black Magic' (maroon), *Heuchera* 'Chocolate Ruffles' (brown foliage), and *Molinia caerulea* 'Edith Dudszus' (an attractive brown grass).

A second way of approaching colour in the garden is to separate the pastel shades from the "hot" colours. In this way of doing things, you have the soft and "tasteful" shades of pale pink, pale yellow, pale blue, and pale mauve on one side, and on the other you have the brash and exciting shades of bright pink, red, bright yellow, bright orange, and so on. Again, divide the garden up according to this idea, and the worst clashes will be avoided. Everyone will admire your taste.

But it adds a touch of individuality to avoid the rules and be inventive if you can. At Sissinghurst I have seen lacy-silvery *Senecio cineraria* planted with the sugar-pink *Verbena* 'Sissinghurst', a sharp little contrast made even more piquant by the addition of the tobacco plant *Nicotiana* 'Lime Green'. Again at Bressingham Gardens, I saw a highly successful orange and pale blue group—the burnt orange crocosmia 'E. A. Bowles' with short yellow heleniums, pale blue agapanthus, *Eryngium* 'Jos Eijking', and purple agastache, all backed by variegated miscanthus. At Bressingham they even get away with

BELOW Silver, lime-green, and sugar-pink making an unusual colour combination at Sissinghurst, Kent, with *Senecio cineraria*, *Verbena* 'Sissinghurst', and *Nicotiana* 'Lime Green'.

BOTTOM You can get away with daring colour clashes if it looks as though you really meant it—the effect shouldn't look like an accident. Dusky pink *Origanum laevigatum* 'Herrenhausen' with orange *Crocosmia* 'Firebird'.

orange *Crocosmia* 'Firebird' with dusky pink *Origanum laevigatum* 'Herrenhausen'.

An exciting scheme that breaks all traditional rules could be made by combining orange, purple, and green: *Kniphofia* 'Shining Sceptre' (orange) beside *Erigeron* 'Dunkelste Aller' (deep violet); *Phlox paniculata* 'Vintage Wine' (purple-red) with *Crocosmia* 'Spitfire' (orange); *Stachys macrantha* 'Hummelo' (purple-red) with *Lychnis* × *arkwrightii* 'Vesuvius' (orange); tender *Verbena* 'Kemerton' (magenta-purple) with *Asclepias tuberosa* (the orange butterfly weed); *Lobelia* × *gerardii* 'Vedrariensis'

BELOW This photo was taken in a garden known for its interesting plant associations, so this startling combination of colours, seemingly lacking in taste, was no doubt intentional and meant to shock. Yes, it's exciting, but no, most of us won't want to copy it.

(purple) with *Crocosmia* 'Constance' (orange)—all mixed with the bold foliage of rodgersias, bergenias, *Helleborus argutifolius*, and *Tetrapanax papyrifer*, and backed by purple-flowered *Clematis* 'Jackmannii'. Daring.

FOLIAGE AND TEXTURE

Foliage colour should be approached with a degree of caution. On the whole, purple-leaved plants blend tolerably well with silver foliage: dark-coloured heucheras and brown-leaved varieties of the dwarf *Geranium sessiliflorum* subsp. *novae-zelandiae* will be acceptable next to santolina or artemisias. Blue foliage, from grasses such as *Helictotrichon semper-virens* and the glaucous leaves of *Dianthus*, blue hostas, *Euphorbia myrsinites*, and *Hebe pinguifolia* 'Pagei', also goes well with silvers. But beware of putting brown directly next to blue-grey, which looks distinctly unpleasant.

Silver always looks better associated with dark green than it does with either brown or blue. *Artemisia* 'Powis Castle' with *Viburnum davidii* makes a sharp and pleasing contrast, almost a black and white theme, which could be continued with *Hedera helix* 'Erecta' beside *Phlomis anatolica* 'Lloyd's Variety'; the curry plant, *Helichrysum italicum*, with clipped box; or *Artemisia alba* 'Canescens' at the base of a dwarf form of *Pinus mugo*. Silver foliage beside variegated foliage is not so good, though it depends on particular cases. Mixing yellow variegation with white-variegated leaves is also doubtful. On the other hand, variegated foliage with dark green works well: *Hakonechloa macra* 'Aureola' with the foliage of *Helleborus foetidus*, for example, or *Euonymus fortunei* 'Silver Queen' beneath *Viburnum tinus*. Yellow leaves, or yellow-variegated foliage, also seem to work well with the yellowy-brown of some grasses—*Stipa capillata*, for example, beneath *Phormium* 'Yellow Wave', or *Carex flagellifera* beside a yellow variegated hosta. However, purple-brown next to yellow is the most problematic. *Physocarpus opulifolius* 'Dart's Gold' with purple phormiums is too strong a contrast, and *Berberis thunbergii* f. *atropurpurea* next to *Filipendula ulmaria* 'Aurea' is also fairly dire.

Of course, green is also a colour, and leaves have shapes and textures too. Effective associations can be made using pale green with dark green; bold foliage next to finely divided; shiny with coarsely textured, and so on. In my own garden I used to have the spikes of a grey-green phormium emerging from the foliage of a Japanese anemone, while nearby was the lacy-textured, blue-green of Jackman's

BELOW A foliage association, created with the use of the huge leaves of *Rheum palmatum* 'Atrosanguineum', variegated irises, *Stachys byzantina* 'Silver Carpet', and the emerging foliage of bronze fennel.

BOTTOM Contrasting foliage effects made with spiky phormiums and the feathery grass *Deschampsia cespitosa* 'Bronzeschleier', mingling with the mauve flower spikes of *Verbena bonariensis*.

foliage association consisting of the huge leaves of *Rheum palmatum* 'Atrosanguineum', the vertical spikes of *Iris pallida* 'Argentea Variegata', *Stachys byzantina* 'Silver Carpet', and the emerging plumes of bronze fennel.

Worthwhile associations featuring contrasting leaf textures might include the rough, dark green leaves of *Crambe cordifolia* next to the shiny silver foliage of the biennial *Eryngium giganteum*. The fuzzy and finely divided heads of the sea lavender *Limonium platyphyllum* 'Violetta' contrast interestingly with the dark solidity of bergenias or *Helleborus argutifolius*. The feathery rounded mass of the grass *Deschampsia cespitosa* 'Bronzeschleier' contrasts well with the spikes of a large phormium, while the neat, dark green leaves of *Hosta* 'Devon Green' are perfect beside the fine green lace of the small umbellifer *Meum athamanticum*. On a much larger scale the delicate, pale blue-green foliage of *Colutea arborescens* would lighten the heaviness and darkness of the thornless holly *Ilex × altaclerensis* 'Camelliifolia'.

REACHING A STYLE

It is clear that, even with the basic "times and conditions" ruling, there still remains a seemingly infinite number of ways of arranging plants together into pleasing associations, whether complementary or contrasting. The next and more challenging stage is to make this a more extensive exercise, involving enough plants to make a whole border. However, we might first ask what style of border we are aiming for. There are plenty of good plants worth trying— the question is, do they fit the look we have in mind?

rue (*Ruta graveolens* 'Jackman's Blue'); then came the rounded dome of a dark green hebe, backed by the arching grassy stems of *Miscanthus sinensis* 'Silberfeder'. All of which gave variety of leaf colour, leaf size and plant shape. At Kew I once saw a good

15
Border style

IF WE ARE HAPPY with an anything-goes border, where anything and everything cohabits in glorious serendipity, then questions of style won't arise. But while chaos and excess are part of the charm of some gardens, they won't do if we have in mind something more focused or disciplined, such as the traditional herbaceous border. Or would a mixed border be a better idea, with year-round interest? Then again, considering the demands of our lifestyle, perhaps we should decide on a low-maintenance, shrubs-and-ground-cover scheme? Are we tempted to try a meadow-like or prairie effect? Would it be more exciting to look exotic? Or would the cottage garden style, in which the most plants are packed into the space that is available , best suit our plant-hoarding tendencies?

THE COTTAGE GARDEN BORDER

In theory, the cottage garden border can absorb almost any plant you care to name, although in practice it favours herbaceous material, with certain plants seen as classic cottage-garden choices. But whatever the plants, the scale of the cottage garden is small and intimate—even if the garden is quite large overall. This is why visitors like Hidcote, in Gloucestershire. Never mind how many acres it covers, the compartments into which it is divided never overwhelm us, and because of this, people can relate to Hidcote, and see its separate "garden rooms" as not too far removed from their own gardens. Hidcote is a garden to visit either on your own, or with one other person. Many of the paths are so narrow that any attempt to be sociable while at the same time admiring the detail of the garden is hopeless, as

you will discover if you agree to go round Hidcote with family and friends. The relationship of the garden to the house at Hidcote is again typical of the cottage garden: there is no relationship to speak of, the garden spaces simply butt up to the house. The same is true at Rodmarton, also in Gloucestershire, where a much larger and grander house has been carefully denied any large or grand spaces in front of it on the garden side.

BELOW The general
profusion of foliage, roses,
and perennials, in various
colours, shapes, and
sizes, in seemingly random
juxtaposition typical of the
cottage garden.

BELOW The inclusion of
useful plants (such as the
angelica seen in the centre
of this photograph), and
a general sense of
organized chaos, are
often characteristic of
the cottage garden.

The overall arrangement of the cottage garden must appear to be artless. Anything contrived or pretentious would not be appreciated. Paths can be straight or crooked, as long as they don't look designed. Artistic curves are *non grata*. There can be little box hedges, but no grand geometry; in fact, a little irregularity is welcome. Asymmetry is fine, but symmetry gone slightly awry would be even better. Borders should bump right up to the house, and lawns should be re-formatted as patches of grass. Beds can be as wide as you like, since the cottage garden is really a vegetable garden that has been taken over by flowers.

Originally these flowers would have been castoffs from the "Great House" where the man of the cottage worked. Many of the flowers seen as typical of the cottage garden are florist's flowers (in other words, flowers for picking), or else they are useful plants such as angelica and other semi-ornamental herbs. Roses have a secure place in the cottage garden, as do lilies, especially *Lilium candidum*, the Madonna lily, emblem of Mary the mother of Jesus. Old-fashioned and fancy primroses, auriculas, streaky tulips, lupins, gypsophila, quaintly marked pinks, violas, rosemary, lavender, sage, and thyme are all part of the cottage garden tapestry. Colour combinations don't stretch beyond immediate neighbours; to subject a whole border to the discipline of a colour scheme would be taking things too far. For

this reason I hesitate to prescribe any plant associations, as this would be to design the un-designed.

Nevertheless, one could imagine an attractive
corner of a cottage garden border where the old, the
common, and the unusual meet—where, for example, the stripey, centuries-old Rosa Mundi rose
(*Rosa gallica* 'Versicolor') grew alongside the tall,
shrubby *Potentilla fruticosa* 'Vilmoriniana' (silver
foliage and pale yellow flowers), along with purple
sage (*Salvia officinalis* 'Purpurascens') and the unusual *Cryptotaenia japonica* f. *atropurpurea*, an
(edible) umbellifer from Japan with dusky purple,
glaucous leaves. Nearby would be *Anchusa azurea*
'Loddon Royalist', which has deep and intensely
blue flowers and coarse foliage, alongside the pale
yellow lupin 'Chandelier' and sweet cicely—*Myrrhis
odorata*—a lacy white umbellifer with medicinal
properties. All these would be interplanted with tall
purple alliums.

Front-row plants to accompany this group would
inevitably include the excellent *Stachys byzantina*,
with its furry leaves ; pinks would be essential, such

as *Dianthus* 'Mrs Sinkins' (white, fluffy-topped, old-fashioned, and top-heavy), 'Dad's Favourite' (an eighteenth-century laced pink, pure white flecked with dark red), or 'Waithman Beauty' (pink-flecked ruby-red). All this could be backed by a wall covered with rambler roses such as 'Albertine', 'Bleu Magenta', or 'Veilchenblau' ("violet-blue"), intermingling with clematis such as 'Etoile Violette' or the dusky-pink 'Hagley Hybrid'.

Another grouping could feature the classic pink rose 'Constance Spry' along with a curious striped rose called 'Camaïeux', dating from about 1830, whose flowers undergo a strange colour change during their three- or four-day life: the flowers start off white, heavily splashed with crimson, but then the stripes fade, first to a magenta colour and finally to light grey. In front of the roses, the grey-leaved dusty miller *Lychnis coronaria* 'Alba' could be grown with *Nepeta subsessilis*, which is a bushy perennial with blue flowers, easily mistaken for a penstemon. Mingling here would be pink and white foxgloves and the double red campion *Silene dioica* 'Flore Pleno'. Front-row plants could include soft pink *Geranium* 'Mavis Simpson', *Gypsophila* 'Giant White', and *Heuchera micrantha* 'Martha Roderick', an early-flowering heuchera with clouds of tiny pink flowers.

One possible drawback of the cottage garden style is that, since summer-flowering herbaceous plants tend to predominate, its period of interest can be limited, and this may not be acceptable for anyone with a small garden. But the situation is no different with the traditional herbaceous border. The main difference between the cottage garden and the

herbaceous border is the degree of discipline imposed. Obviously the herbaceous border concentrates on perennials, but it also accepts a greater degree of control over colours, shapes, and heights. Also, its setting within the garden is different. Whereas the cottage garden might only offer a one-person path, where you might almost feel you are in among the plants, the herbaceous border usually has a wide path beside it, inviting the viewer to stand back and admire the border as a whole, or at least the association of various plants together. However, if excessive order and discipline is not to one's taste, an alternative style that may have appeal is the meadow garden.

THE MEADOW STYLE

The meadow style comes in various permutations, from large fields sown with wildflowers to a selection of tough perennials holding their own in long grass. However, a meadow effect can be created in a border without all the bother of having a real meadow, with its inevitable weeds and mowing regimes. With the right choice of plants, its care need be no different from that of any other border.

A meadow has three principal characteristics. First, it has a large number of grasses in it (none variegated, and none standing more than waist-high); secondly, it features a limited number of plants which repeat randomly; and thirdly, a high proportion of the plants that give it colour are likely to be either daisy-flowered or umbelliferous.

Following these principles, we can proceed to make our "meadow effect" border. The taller plants could include a wonderful range of specimen grasses,

such as *Melica altissima*, very unpretentious but with good flower heads; *Stipa gigantea*, the giant oat grass; and *Calamagrostis × acutiflora* 'Karl Foerster', an excellent and very upright plant. Two other good grasses better grown in groups or long bands rather than as specimens are *Calamagrostis brachytricha*, nicely arching with a hint of bronze to the flower-head, and *Stipa calamagrostis*—somewhat similar, but with whiter heads.

Tall perennials to grow with these could include the cream-coloured daisies of *Anthemis tinctoria* 'Sauce Hollandaise', or the yellow ones of 'E. C. Buxton'; *Boltonia asteroides* 'Snowbank', an *Aster* relative with a delicate mass of of daisy flowers in late summer; echinaceas, such as the reddish-purple *E.* 'Robert Bloom', three feet (90 cm) tall, or 'White

Swan', greyish white and slightly shorter at two feet (60 cm); cranesbills such as *Geranium pratense* cultivars, or *G. sylvaticum* 'Amy Doncaster'; a Shasta daisy such as *Leucanthemum × superbum* 'Snow Lady'; a poppy such as scarlet *Papaver orientale* 'Ladybird'; *Persicaria amplexicaulis* 'Atrosanguinea'; and the so-called "queen of the umbellifers", *Selinum wallichianum*. Crucially, note what has been left off the list: anything well-groomed, exotic, too "gardenish" or highly bred, such as a double hybrid peony.

Grasses growing to a medium size could include fuzzy-floppy, golden-haired *Stipa tenuissima*; stiffly vertical *Molinia caerulea* 'Edith Dudszus', which turns a beautiful buff-bronze colour; *Miscanthus sinensis* 'Yakushima Dwarf', probably the only miscanthus short enough for our purpose; and the fluffy pom-pom heads of *Pennisetum alopecuroides* and *P. orientale*, the two hardiest pennisetums, both deserving a place on the front row in spite of their height. In between these grasses one could grow *Achillea ptarmica* 'The Pearl'; astrantias, such as the silvery-green *A. major* subsp. *involucrata* 'Shaggy' or silvery-pink *A.* 'Buckland'; yellow *Coreopsis verticillata* daisies; *Echinops ritro*, the nearest we might want to get to a thistle, with grey foliage and silvery-blue globe-thistle heads; the rarely seen *Kalimeris pinnatifida*, an easy-to-grow Japanese *Aster* relative with white daisies; dark red, wild-scabious-like *Knautia macedonica*; the artless yellow *Patrinia scabiosifolia* 'Nagoya', which looks a little like an umbellifer but is actually in the valerian family;

BELOW The meadow effect created on a small scale in an average-sized country garden. A wide range of grasses, and perennials, including (daisy-flowered) anthemis, verbascums, and species delphiniums.

BOTTOM *Stipa calamagrostis* and *Gaura lindheimeri* 'Siskiyou Pink', with *Calamagrostis × acutiflora* Karl Foerster, in late summer.

Pimpinella major 'Rosea', a pink form of the burnet saxifrage distantly related to cow-parsley; *Smyrnium olusatrum* (alexanders, the parsley from Alexandria), a yellow umbellifer with many culinary uses, good in winter and spring, but not so good in summer; and

bright yellow rudbeckias. Eminently suitable asters for late in the season are *A. divaricatus*, with an airy display of white aster-daisies on two feet (60 cm) stems, and *A. lateriflorus* 'Prince', with tiny pale pink flowers. *Achillea* cultivars would echo the wild yarrow of field and hedgerow; one could try pale sherbert-yellow 'Anthea' or, more adventurously, 'Terracotta'. But achillea plants don't seem to last long and need propagating every two or three years.

Lower-growing grasses could include *Carex testacea* and other small brownish-green carexes, along with small festucas, and even *Miscanthus oligostachyus* 'Nanus Variegatus'—not strongly variegated, but good in a band along the front of the border. Seslerias would also be worth investigating. With these one could grow the white daisies of *Anthemis punctata* subsp. *cupaniana*; the white umbellifer *Meum athamanticum*, supposedly called spignel or baldmoney; and small geraniums such as *G. sanguineum* 'Album' or pink 'Glenluce', along with the various fillers-in mentioned in Chapter 10 (see pages 110–123), such as *Lamium galeobdolon* 'Silberteppich' and 'Hermann's Pride', and *Geranium × cantabrigiense* 'St. Ola' or 'Karmina'.

To assemble a border with this range of plants to hand, one could start by making a carpet of dwarf geraniums and lamiums in the manner described in Chapter 10 (see pages 120–3). Along the front row could go long ribbons of *Carex testacea* and *Miscanthus oligostachyus* 'Nanus Variegatus', with dwarf geraniums also taking turns at the front, and perhaps *Stipa tenuissima* as a small feature plant to break the line. Into this carpet we could set our first plant group: the melick grass *Melica altissima* with

Anthemis tinctoria 'Sauce Hollandaise', and *Calamagrostis × acutiflora* 'Karl Foerster' with *Echinacea purpurea* 'Robert Bloom'. In front of these would go *Pimpinella major* 'Rosea' interplanted with *Knautia macedonica*, followed by the grass *Molinia caerulea* 'Edith Dudszus', then *Astrantia* 'Buckland' with a long band of *Calamagrostis brachytricha*.

The next group, still planted in the same basic carpet, could begin with *Pennisetum alopecuroides* breaking into the front row, with yellow *Coreopsis verticillata* next to silver-blue *Echinops ritro*, and the late-flowering *Patrinia scabiosifolia* 'Nagoya' beside *Miscanthus sinensis* 'Yakushima Dwarf'. *Smyrnium olusatrum* could sit behind a band of *Stipa calamagrostis*. Taller plants behind these would be *Boltonia asteroides* 'Snowbank', *Persicaria amplexicaulis* 'Atrosanguinea', and *Selinum wallichianum*.

With so many grasses and wild-looking things, this would give us the meadow effect we are looking for. The emphasis would be very much on mid- to late summer, but this is inevitable with so many perennials in the scheme. Apart from a burst of clearing-up activity in the spring, such a border is not particularly difficult to look after, but if we are looking for more year-round interest, or a border needing even less maintenance, other approaches may be more appropriate.

THE LABOUR-SAVING BORDER

If the amount of time we have for gardening is limited, we may need to restrict the plants we choose to those which are reasonably work-free. This can be arranged with the aid of some of the ground-cover plants discussed in Chapter 10, along with other easy-care perennials. Small shrubs can also be used, avoiding the large flowering shrubs that will create work by growing too big.

Our first grouping, for a labour-saving border in a sunny position, might begin with the excellent foliage shrub *Viburnum davidii*, planted beside *Cistus × purpureus*, with a mass of pink flowers in early summer and grey foliage that contrasts effectively with the dark green of the viburnum. (To get the blue berries on the viburnum in the autumn, another plant of *V. davidii* will be needed somewhere in the garden, since male and female flowers occur on separate plants.) With these one could plant *Sambucus nigra* 'Thundercloud', an elder with pinkish-red flowers in May-June and dark red-black foliage that will complement the darkness of the viburnum leaf, and contrast again with the grey cistus. The elder might grow rather fast, but it will take cutting back, and its soft wood makes it very easy to prune.

BELOW The contrasting
shapes and forms of *Fatsia
japonica*, a Pfitzer juniper,
and lyme grass, *Leymus
arenarius*, creating an almost
maintenance-free grouping
at Hounslow Civic Centre.
Planting designed by
Preben Jakobsen.

In front of these three shrubs there would be scope for at least five or six perennials or smaller shrubs. To pick up the silver-grey theme, *Artemisia arborescens* would be a good choice—a wonderfully airy, lacy, silver-leaved perennial, though not as hardy as the shorter and more widely seen *A*. 'Powis Castle'. To continue the theme of the pink umbellifer-like flowerheads of the *Sambucus*, one could plant *Filipendula purpurea*, an ornamental meadowsweet that performs well in any soil that is not too dry. Hopefully the flowers would coincide, though the elder might well get ahead. An ideal companion for the meadowsweet would be *Geranium sylvaticum* 'Album', a "good do-er" of Persil whiteness. Later one could have pinkish-red penstemons, such as 'Elmley', 'Rich Ruby', or 'Patio Wine', and it might not be too much effort to cut down the spent flowerheads to promote further flowering. We could continue the silver theme with the upward-curving

stems of *Phlomis italica*, adding colour with a modern daylily such as *Hemerocallis* 'Borgia Queen', or one of the "spider" types such as 'Dancing Summerbird' or 'Lilting Lavender'. Some of these perennials, such as the phlomis and the daylily, could take front-row positions; other drifts of front-row plants could include a white helianthemum, the dwarf grey shrub *Hebe pimeleioides* 'Quicksilver', and *Geranium* 'Philippe Vapelle'. To break up the soft roundedness of this grouping, it would be possible to insert among these front-row carpeters the vertical stems of *Iris pallida* 'Argentea Variegata', or the khaki spikes of *Libertia peregrinans*.

None of these plants would create much of a workload, apart from tidying up at the beginning and end of the season. Once the plants are established there will be little room for weeds to take hold, especially considering that the ground would be fairly well covered during the winter.

Of course, not all borders enjoy sun, and many smaller town gardens suffer from being shady due to the proximity of trees or nearby buildings. For a shade-tolerant, easy-care plant association, one could begin with *Mahonia aquifolium* 'Smaragd' (which means "emerald"), 'Apollo', or 'Atropurpurea', all with slightly glossy, prickly-edged leaves and yellow flowers in spring. To brighten up the darkness that many shady areas have, one could plant the yellow-leaved *Berberis thunbergii* 'Aurea' and white-variegated *Euonymus fortunei* 'Silver Queen'. The dominant feature could be *Fatsia japonica*, a wonderful architectural plant that flourishes in the dense shade of buildings. Eventually it reaches eight or even ten feet (2.5 or 3 m) in all directions, but forms an open canopy with foliage only at the top, supported on long arching stems. Many shade-loving plants would grow happily beneath it. Among evergreen ferns, it's hard to improve on

Polystichum setiferum cultivars such as those in the Divisilobum Group, though the overwintering *Dryopteris erythrosora* would be a close rival. Easy-care grasses such as *Hakonechloa macra* 'Aureola', *Carex oshimensis* 'Evergold', and *Carex* 'Silver Sceptre' could be planted among the ferns, along with carpets of variegated ivy, symphytums, and epimediums. One could add *Euphorbia robbiae* as long as the soil was not too light, in which case the spurge might spread too fast and become a nuisance. More exciting low-level plants could be used, but work tends to increase with interest. *Aruncus dioicus*, for example, is cited as both shade-tolerant and ground-covering, but it forms a very large herbaceous plant, and somebody will have to cut down all that tough foliage at the end of the season and get rid of it. Similarly, hostas are often listed as ground-cover plants, but they're necessarily attention-dependent as well. Someone has to remember to keep the slugs at bay, otherwise there will be no hostas. Similarly bergenias can't be recommended for the no-work garden, since they will look an untidy mess if no-one is prepared to spend time tidying them up twice a year, taking out the dead leaves and picking off the dead flowerheads. Arguably, even hellebores need tidying up. But if you crave more glamour, it's difficult to see that an arisaema such as *A. candidissimum*, growing in a patch of *Adiantum venustum*, would create much work.

THE EXOTIC BORDER

As a break from the conventional garden scene, we might decide to create a more exotic effect, as if the garden belonged to the subtropics instead of the

mild temperate part of the world. This can be
achieved by limiting one's choices to plants with
large glossy leaves, spiky foliage, or some other
kind of strong character.

Around the edges of the exotic garden one might
want to include the large leathery leaves of the
loquat *Eriobotrya japonica*; a fig tree (*Ficus carica*);
the large glossy-leaved *Magnolia grandiflora*; *Fatsia
japonica* (again); prickly *Mahonia japonica*; or mini-
jungles of bamboos.

Small trees could include Japanese maples (*Acer
palmatum*); the devil's walking-stick, *Aralia elata*;
tree ferns such as *Dicksonia antarctica*; the so-called
golden rain tree, *Koelreuteria paniculata*; *Magnolia
× soulangeana*; and one of the *Rhus* species such as
common sumach (*Rhus typhina*) or the more unusual
Rhus trichocarpa. Shrubs could include *Daphni-
phyllum himalaense* subsp. *macropodum* (a distant
euphorbia relative, often listed as plain *D. macropodum*); hydrangeas such as *H. aspera*, its subspecies

sargentiana or its relatives in the Villosa Group (as long as they're in a sheltered position); the quintessentially exotic-looking rice-paper plant *Tetrapanax papyrifer*; *Viburnum davidii*; and arching, jungly roses such as *Rosa moyesii*.

Other feature plants could include some striking perennials with good foliage, such as cardoons (*Cynara cardunculus*), *Euphorbia characias*, the massive *Heracleum mantegazzianum*, silvery-blue-green *Melianthus major*, and *Macleaya cordata*. On moist ground, the exotic look can be emphasized with large-leaved *Astilboides tabularis*, *Darmera peltata*, gunneras, ligularias, and *Rodgersia podophylla* and *R. pinnata*. Elsewhere, spiky plants to enhance the effect include astelias (if you have a Zone 9 climate), *Kniphofia caulescens* (which dislikes winter wet), and of course, phormiums and yuccas. Less formidable spikes include *Iris foetidissima* (plain or variegated), *Iris pallida* 'Variegata', and libertias.

Ferns would fit in well, such as *Asplenium scolopendrium*, *Athyrium felix-femina* Plumosum Group, *Dryopteris wallichiana*, the Prince-of-Wales-feathers fern *Matteuccia*, and evergreen *Polystichum aculeatum* and *P. setiferum* 'Pulcherrimum Bevis'. The strong-charactered grasses could also be added, such as *Chionochloa rubra*, cortaderias, *Carex buchananii*, miscanthus, and *Stipa arundinacea* and *S. gigantea*. Suitable flowering perennials could include *Acanthus mollis*, eryngiums, *Euphorbia griffithii*, *E. palustris* and *E. mellifera*, fennel (*Foeniculum*, a self-seeder), *Geranium maderense*, other kniphofias, *Helleborus argutifolius* and *H. foetidus*, hemerocallis, and *Zantedeschia*.

THE MIXED BORDER

The styles of planting discussed above all rely to a degree on "top-down" thinking—in other words, one decides on a particular "look" for the border first and then chooses the plants with which to achieve it. But limiting plant choice for stylistic reasons may not appeal to the plant collector. Thus, an alternative approach would be an exercise in "bottom-up" thinking; devising a less restrictive scheme in which all our favourites, whatever they might be, could cohabit happily and be displayed to best advantage. For the eclectic plant collector, the mixed border is perhaps the most useful style, attempting to offer interest all the year around, having some similarities to the cottage garden, but with a little more law and order introduced here and there. The ideas that can lift such a scheme from random juxtaposition to art, however, need a whole new chapter to explore.

16
Border strategy

THE BEST PRACTICAL STATEGY for planning a border, whether on the ground or on paper, is to put the high-impact plants in position first, followed by the evergreen or over-wintering plants. Around these main players, the "fillers", or smaller flowering plants, can be arranged. However, before we plunge into this enterprise in any detail, it is worth making some basic observations about borders.

ARISTOTLE SAYS

Aristotle is often quoted as saying that a play should have a beginning, a middle, and an end, and the literary critics of posterity have taken the view that this remark (which you might have thought was obvious) was rather profound. Let me, then, make the equally profound statement that borders have fronts, backs, and middles. We have already observed in Chapter 14 (see pages 163–4) that one plant can be seen as the background to another; that a tall *Eremurus* or foxtail lily, for example, will show up better if it has an evergreen shrub behind it rather than a distracting mixture of different colours and shapes. This principle applies equally to the border as a whole: the entire scheme needs a background. In addition, all the plants at the back of the border, individually or as a group, can be thought of as the background to the plants at the front.

Many a classic English herbaceous border was set in front of a clipped yew hedge, not on the basis of whim or tradition, but because the dark, plain, smooth texture of the yew made the perfect background for flowering plants. Among a hundred and one places where this can be seen is Rodmarton in Gloucestershire, and it's worth noting that in the

Red Border at Hidcote, also in Gloucestershire, the plants on the upper side of the garden, which have a tall yew hedge behind them, show up slightly better than the plants on the lower side, which don't. Many other evergreen shrubs can be used instead of yew; as we saw when looking at shrubs in Chapter 9 (see pages 102), *Itea ilicifolia* could work well, being not only interesting in itself at times (mildly prickly foliage and yellow tassel-catkins in midsummer), but

BELOW A large mixed
border at Holehird, near
Windermere, Cumbria,
with a wide range of
shrubs, roses, grasses,
and perennials, closely
associated and pleasingly
graded in height.

BELOW The famous
Red Border at Hidcote, in
Gloucestershire. The smooth,
dark green surface of the
yew hedge is an essential
element of the scheme,
providing a plain back
ground for the restless
shapes and primary colours.

feet (30 by 10 m) in size and divided by a path about six feet (1.8 m) wide, running down the centre. At the back of the borders she shows a clipped tamarisk hedge, to provide a smooth, neutral background that would set off the perennials to advantage.

FOREGROUNDS

At the front of two borders a hundred feet (30 m) long, one might expect Jekyll's plan to show a wide range of different and interesting small plants. At close range they would look fine, but when seen from a distance, especially with the critical eye of Miss Jekyll, the overall result might have been disappointing. One of this. One of that. A spot of pink, a dot of red, a little splash of yellow, and so on, in restless succession.

It seems that Gertrude Jekyll thought that the front edge of the border was a place where restraint was needed. The edges of her path feature just five different plants: stachys, *Senecio cineraria* (formerly

also creating that darkish green background. Other good candidates are osmanthus, *Viburnum tinus*, or almost any slow-growing evergreen.

Photographs of Gertrude Jekyll's gardens indicate that she knew all about this back-front-and-middle rule, and the plans of her border designs reprinted in *Colour Schemes for the Flower Garden*[5] show how she tackles this issue. A good example is her design for a Grey Garden, which is a hundred by thirty-five

Cineraria maritima), pinks, santolina, and catmint. When each long, narrow drift of one plant averages twenty feet (6 m) in length, she isn't exactly giving in to excessive horticultural inclusiveness. Miss Jekyll's Blue Garden shows exactly the same approach, with a fifteen-feet (4.5-m) run of *Hosta sieboldiana*, for example, and so does her Green Garden, where she has a twenty-feet (6-m) band of epimediums and the same length of *Asarum europaeum*.

These long drifts in the foreground create a firm base line for the border, performing a similar function to the background. In the case of the Grey Garden, they create a cool, silvery setting for the contrasting colours, shapes, and textures of the plants behind. In all of these schemes, strong accent plants such as yuccas, acanthus, or the tall spires of hollyhocks or delphiniums ensure that there is plenty happening in the middle of the border. In the Grey Garden the mid-border area is a tastefully controlled jungle: cranesbill geraniums, *Echinops*, lilies, yuccas, achilleas, *Leymus* (Lyme grass), and more. There is no need for yet more contrast and restlessness along the front edge, as this would only distract the eye. Just as a plain vase is all a good flower arrangement needs, so restrained planting along the front of the border often looks best. But as someone who likes to maximize the number of different plants I can grow, I admit this restraint is not easy to adhere to in a small garden.

When choosing plants for the foreground of the border, one also needs to consider the scale of the border as a whole: the front-row plants need to be appropriate in size for the rest of the bed. If there are very large plants towards the back of the border, the foreground planting will look out of proportion if the plants are completely prostrate. Acaenas, ajugas, lamiums, or waldsteinia, all of which hug the ground, will be too small in comparison with the rest of the border. As a rough guide, plants along the front of an average border of tall perennials need to be at least six inches (15 cm) high, although one can get away with carpeters that are taller when in flower, such as *Saxifraga* × *urbium* (London pride) or *Persicaria affinis* 'Darjeeling Red'. Prostrate plants can be used successfully in narrow borders that don't contain anything very tall—or with an intermediate plant, about eighteen inches (45 cm) high, behind the low one to bridge the gap.

BORDERS AGAINST GRAVEL

The surface that runs alongside the front of the border may well affect the choice of front-line plants. Different plants have to be selected depending on whether there is a lawn, a gravel path, or paving beside the border. Gravel and paving are easy to work with: plants can creep forward without getting

in the way of a mower, and bare patches of soil can be avoided. Many plants enjoy the warmth and dryness that gravel and paving provide, especially those that are slightly succulent, such as sedums, *Euphorbia myrsinites* and *E. rigida*, and *Othonna cheirifolia* (a subshrub with grey leaves like cat's tongues and yellow daisy flowers, intolerant of winter wet).

Many silver-leaved plants prefer the dry, warm surface that a gravel or paved surface provides them. When it comes to stachys, or lamb's ears, I prefer the old-fashioned species *Stachys byzantina*, which flowers—in contrast to the dreary flowerless cultivar 'Silver Carpet', which so many nurseries offer for sale. Later in the season, however, stachys can "go off" in appearance due to mildew, especially older plants, though this doesn't tend to be a problem in cooler climates.

Artemisias are good plants against gravel or paving: little *A. schmidtiana* 'Nana', three to six

BELOW LEFT
Artemisias, such as *A. eriantha,* associate well with gravel, perhaps used as an ornamental mulch or as a gravel path.

BELOW RIGHT
Sedums, such as *S. telephium* 'Matrona', enjoy the warmth and the dry surface provided by gravel.

OPPOSITE A pink and white border edged with gravel at Holehird, in Cumbria, in Northern England.

inches (8 to 15 cm) tall, forms beautiful, bumpy, creeping cushions of dense silver filigree. Another good artemisia, though rarely seen, is *A. eriantha* (syn. *A. villarsii*), a similar silvery colour to *A. alba* 'Canescens', but with a slightly denser and more upright habit, about ten to twelve inches (25 to 30 cm) high. *Artemisia frigida* is an attractive silvery species, up to twenty inches (50 cm) in height, while *A. caucasica* (syn. *A. pedemontana*) is shorter but slightly more upright, up to twelve inches (30 cm) tall. Some plants formerly known as artemisias are now being called *Seriphidium*, although the difference might seem invisible to gardeners. *Seriphidium maritimum* forms a pleasing mound of silver-grey, usually eighteen inches (45 cm) in height, although apparently it can grow much taller. *Seriphidium vallesiacum* is a whiter shade of silver, again eighteen inches (45 cm) high when cultivated, but capable of three times that height in the wild.

A good argument could be made that *Anthemis punctata* subsp. *cupaniana* has more to offer than any of these artemisias. Its foliage is just as silvery, but instead of insignificant greyish flowers, the anthemis puts on an extrovert display of white daisies with yellow centres. Although the flowers are not quite in the A-class, they are cheerful, and appear quite early—from late spring—and make a good setting for bulbs. Each plant will form a spreading mat of foliage twelve inches (30 cm) high and often three feet (90 cm) wide. Like the artemisias, it needs a good tidy-up periodically, but soon recovers.

Other silvery plants to grow alongside gravel or paving are dianthus, helianthemums, *Cerastium tomentosum* var. *columnae*, and limoniums. A nepeta such as 'Six Hills Giant' is especially good for toning down hot and brash colours, or for the edges of beds of brightly coloured hybrid tea roses. *Veronica spicata* subsp. *incana* has silvery foliage and violet-blue

flower spikes, about twelve inches (30 cm) high, with many good cultivars such as 'Sahin's Early'.

Among suitable sedums for this situation are *Sedum* 'Herbstfreude' (say "*hairpst-froyda*"), a reliable performer often known as 'Autumn Joy'. Its flat, dark red heads last from August right into the winter; even after they have died they can be appreciated as examples of "beautiful death syndrome". Other good sedums are 'Joyce Henderson' (slightly taller, with pink flowers and a purple flush to the leaves); *Sedum telephium* 'Matrona' (good autumnal foliage colours, pinkish flowers); *S. telephium* subsp. *ruprechtii* (cream flowers, pink-tinged leaves, twelve inches/30 cm high); 'Stewed Rhubarb Mountain' (white flowers from pink buds, in mounding heads, twelve inches/30 cm high); along with the *Sedum spectabile* cultivars 'Stardust' (white flowers), 'Indian Chief' (maroon), and 'Meteor' (purple), all fourteen to sixteen inches (35 to 40 cm) high.

BORDERS AGAINST GRASS

A lawn running alongside a border is very commonly seen, but is not as easy to manage as gravel or paving. To have a small patch of bare earth between the grass and the first row of plants can look awkward; it has to be constantly weeded and creates a little vertical edge that has to be trimmed every time the lawn is mown. One solution is to have a mowing strip, at least one brick wide (nine inches/23 cm), which eliminates trimming and allows plants to flop forward without getting entangled in the mower. This is a rather architectural solution, suitable near the house or in a fairly formal part of the garden; it might look wrong further out in the garden. Nor will it be appropriate if the style of the entire garden is to be naturalistic.

Another way to avoid the "ledge-and-bare-earth" scenario is to select edging plants that you can mow right up to. If the right plants are chosen, a rotary

mower can reach under their overhanging stems without harming them. Some shrubs make this fairly easy to achieve—for example, *Sarcococca hookeriana* var. *humilis*, *Lonicera pileata*, dwarf shrubby potentillas, or dwarf cistus, such as *C.* × *dansereaui* 'Decumbens' or *C. salviifolius* 'Prostratus'. Hebes are to be avoided, as they don't recover well from any accidental damage.

Perennials in this position have to be tough enough to stop the grass encroaching into the border, and the ones to choose are either in the ground-cover category, or those listed as suitable for naturalizing. Hemerocallis are fine early on, while they are holding their stems up, but later in the season some intervention may be necessary to prevent flopping leaves getting into the mower. Other perennials worth trying against grass are epimediums, astilbes, persicarias, symphytums, liriopes, *Iris foetidissima*, and the Pacific Coast irises, or Californian Hybrids, as we should

now call them, such as 'Banbury Beauty' (although many good examples seem to circulate unnamed among devotees). Smaller grasses and sedges can also work well, especially carexes such *C. oshimensis* 'Evergold', *C. testacea*, and *C. morrowii* cultivars.

Many of the slightly taller grasses are also suitable for placing alongside a lawn, such as *Calamagrostis brachytricha*, blue *Elymus magellanicus*, *Festuca mairei*, *Hakonechloa macra* 'Aureola', pennisetums, and *Stipa calamagrostis*. A front-of-border position is always advantageous for grasses with a good arching habit, so that their shape can be seen to advantage. Any miscanthus could be used, although the shorter ones would be best. *Deschampsia cespitosa* cultivars are also best at the front of the border, in spite of their height, because it allows their full feathery effect to be appreciated without other plants crowding in. On the other hand, their foliage early in the season is unimpressive; they are nothing worth noticing until at least midsummer. It is important that ornamental grasses are properly established before there is any relaxation of the weeding and trimming regime along the front of the border. Trying to get grassy weeds disentangled from the roots of ornamental grasses is a tedious process.

There are a few herbaceous plants with small leaves that can be used against grass, since there are some whose leaves can be cut or damaged without spoiling the appearance of the plant. In this category are smaller geraniums such as *G. sanguineum* 'Album', dicentras, and *Alchemilla conjuncta*. Perennials with larger leaves are more problematic: hostas, rodgersias, acanthus, and the larger-leafed bergenias are all vulnerable to damage by the

could be used as long as one is prepared to keep cutting off stems that droop on to the grass—and there always seem to be a few.

The front of the border is also a good place for feature plants, or anything which looks best as a specimen. *Kniphofia caulescens*, *Artemisia* 'Powis Castle', *Chionochloa rubra*, and *Libertia peregrinans* fall into this category, along with *Acanthus mollis* and the Corsican hellebore *Helleborus argutifolius*. Perovskia, yuccas, and phormiums with an arching habit can also be grown in this way. The stiff, spiky phormiums can go further back.

THE MIXED BORDER

The herbaceous border concentrates its efforts on the summer months, and this always seems impressive to the one-time summer visitor. But if we return earlier the next year, perhaps in late spring, we may well be disappointed to discover that all there is to admire is emerging greenery. Our only comfort might be that had it been February, there might have been nothing to be seen at all. But with the mixed border, the aim is to provide greater continuity of interest. The summer profusion of colour will necessarily be reduced, but you can't have everything. To make a mixed border demands a multi-season strategy: what will there be to look at in January or in March? What will there be to see (dare you ask) in November? Unlike stylistic ideas such as the meadow garden or the exotic look, discussed in the previous chapter, the mixed border is not a "look" or style with distinctive features: rather, it is simply a way of trying to look interesting and respectable all the year around.

mower. Most euphorbias are also to be avoided, except perhaps *E. robbiae*, since their milky stems get into an unpleasant mess if the mower strays too close and chews them up. *Euphorbia characias*

such as *S. ruscifolia* var. *chinensis* (with sharply pointed dark green leaves and small, white, scented flowers in late winter). In my own garden I have *Olearia nummularifolia* rubbing shoulders happily with perennials. Not-very-thorny hollies could be used: *Ilex aquifolium* 'J. C. van Tol' or, if variegation is acceptable, *Ilex × altaclerensis* 'Lawsoniana', which is an excellent yellow-splashed cultivar. Both of these hollies are female and therefore berry-bearing. For winter flowers, a mahonia would be invaluable. Smaller types of evergreen might include a cistus, a rosemary, and a hebe or two.

To accompany the evergreen shrubs there are several perennials with overwintering foliage. Top of the list might well come *Euphorbia characias*, of which subsp. *wulfenii* 'Lambrook Gold' is a difficult cultivar to beat. Additional winter foliage can be provided by dianthus, evergreen eryngiums, iberis, penstemons, kniphofias, *Helleborus argutifolius*, *Heuchera* 'Mint Frost', or a bergenia such as 'Abendglocken', 'Oeschberg', or any good form of *Bergenia purpurascens*.

Flowers for late winter and for early spring would have to include hellebores, both the hybrids and *H. argutifolius* (again) for its pale green blooms, along with the winter-flowering irises *I. unguicularis* and *I. lazica*, and pulmonarias. Bulbs could include *Crocus tommasinianus* (supposing we wanted these in the border), *Anemone blanda*, and a reliable short-stemmed *Narcissus* such as 'Jumblie'.

For late spring, euphorbias would be essential (again), along with perennial wallflowers, dicentras, helianthemums (evergreen), iberis, and the bearded irises. Moving into the early summer season we

Stage one, as we know, will be to establish the architectural plants, and then the plants for winter interest, as these will form the "bones" of the scheme. We shall need a selection of evergreen shubs that are not too large, such as *Phlomis anatolica* 'Lloyd's Variety' (a good Jerusalem sage), and sarcococcas

through the whole bed, to get a balanced coverage of greenery from October to May. The other material can then be clustered in seasonal groups: three mid-summer plants here, followed by three or four late summer/autumn plants there, followed in turn by two or three early spring plants, and so on.

We might start with *Phlomis anatolica* 'Lloyd's Variety' as one of the evergreen shrubs dotted along the border. In front of this we could have a group of three summer-flowering plants: pale mauvey-blue *Penstemon* 'Sour Grapes' (evergreen in mild areas), *Fuchsia magellanica* var. *gracilis* 'Tricolor' (with a long period of foliage interest), and the pale pink *Geranium* × *riversleaianum* 'Mavis Simpson'. Linking in with this scheme, we could follow on with the deep pink Japanese anemone *A. hupehensis* 'Bowles' Pink' (also with good foliage over a long period), with the spikes of *Acanthus mollis* for a bit more impact. Behind these could be the white-variegated *Kerria japonica* 'Picta' (often labelled 'Variegata'), picking up the variegation of the fuchsia and giving us some flowers in late spring.

Next would come something softer in texture to follow the strong acanthus: *Aster* × *frikartii* 'Flora's Delight' (about half the height of the sometimes willowy 'Mönch'), with a band of silver *Stachys byzantina* in front of it. To follow this we would have a band of bergenias along the front, with a tall *Euphorbia characias* towards the back, such as 'Thelma's Giant' (both giving us evergreen coverage, and flowers early in the season). The space between the two would be taken up by the pink *Geranium sanguineum* 'Alan Bloom' and the ever-flexible *Malva moschata* f. *alba*.

reach peony time, along with the oriental poppies, aquilegias, geraniums, daylilies, alchemillas, and alstroemerias. Selected roses that blend with other kinds of planting could not be omitted from the mixed border.

For summer the best choices are perennials that flower over a long period: penstemons, persicarias, *Acanthus mollis*, coreopsis, solidagos, and heleniums. Competing for our attention along with these will be kniphofias, eryngiums, phlox, macleaya, *Malva moschata* f. *alba*, rudbeckias, and *Echinacea purpurea*, perhaps interspersed with the best grasses. Into autumn there will still be plenty to enjoy: the Michaelmas daisies and other *Aster* species and cultivars, along with Japanese anemones and, eventually, a few chrysanthemums.

PUTTING IT ALL TOGETHER

The technique of creating the mixed border is to mix the evergreen shrubs and overwintering perennials

BELOW Lively colours and shapes in a mixed planting scheme at Rosemoor, in North Devon, with shrubs and trees, tender and hardy perennials, including *Hypericum*, *Euphorbia palustris*, dahlias, and herbaceous potentillas.

BOTTOM Evergreen perennials, such as the Corsican hellebore, *H. argutifolius*, are particularly useful in the border for the foliage they provide during the winter months.

Helleborus argutifolius, evergreen and elegant, would then come to the front row, followed by *Geranium × cantabrigiense* 'Karmina', compact and pink, forming a base for about thirty *Narcissus* 'Jumblie'. Behind these would be a late summer group: the yellow spikes of *Kniphofia* 'Percy's Pride', the grass *Calamagrostis × acutiflora* 'Karl Foerster', and deep pink *Echinacea purpurea* 'Robert Bloom', all backed by the blue-grey-green foliage of *Macleaya cordata*.

Next in line beside the macleaya would be a tall *Miscanthus sinensis* cultivar, such as 'Kaskade' or

BELOW Gentle, pastel colours, plenty of foliage interest, and beautifully graded heights make this a very satisfying border, at Bourton House, near Moreton in Marsh, Gloucestershire.

'Graziella', with a sarcococca in front, such as *S. confusa* (our next evergreen shrub), side by side with the silver foliage of *Lotus hirsutus* (ever-grey) and the blue *Geranium* 'Rozanne' (long-flowering), and *Sedum* 'Joyce Henderson' (foliage flushed purple, pink flowers) with *Persicaria affinis* 'Donald Lowndes' along the front row. The line could be broken by bringing forward the hardy evergreen *Phormium* 'Sundowner' (variegated leaves in shades of dark green and bronze-pink) almost to the front, with *Geranium macrorrhizum* 'Bevan's Variety' (bright pink flowers) at its base. Beside the phormium, and giving it a plain background as the border is viewed along its length, could be the rounded shape and delicate texture of *Hebe cupressoides* (evergreen), with *Alchemilla conjuncta* (silvery-edged leaves) and starry-blue *Anemone blanda* at its base. Behind all this would be the arching stems of *Rosa glauca* (mauve foliage, pink flowers, red hips). And so the mixed border would go on, ensuring there was always something in the depths of winter, and giving a nod to every season along its length.

17
Integrating the single-genus collection

THE IDEAS AND OBSERVATIONS in the previous chapters can be used by the general, or eclectic, plant collector, or any keen gardener, but what about the specialist who wants to mix and match the plants of a single genus among the beds and borders? It may be useful, therefore, to look at three very different collections, taking seemingly random examples, and see how they could be associated with other plants in the border. For the sake of argument we will try out *Heliopsis*, *Arum*, and a joint collection of dwarf conifers from *Thuja* and *Platycladus*, the powers that be having fairly recently decided that *Thuja orientalis* must now be called *Platycladus orientalis*.

LIKE THE SUN

First we need to ask what kind of plants heliopsis are, and what conditions will suit them best. The genus *Heliopsis* is a member of the Compositae, the daisy family (although some botanists prefer to call this the Asteraceae); it consists of leafy perennials, whose cultivars are grown for their flowers. The foliage is of an average green colour and is neither remarkable nor objectionable. The flowers are bright yellow, about two to three inches (5 to 8 cm) across; they may be single or double, and occur on the top fifth of the plant's height. *Heliopsis* are not specimen plants or stand-alone feature plants, but socializers that are happy to benefit from companions in a border. They are three to four feet (90 to 120 cm) high, forming clumps about twenty-four inches (60 cm) across. As this makes a single plant taller than it is wide, we would do well to decide to plant two or three of each kind together, about eighteen inches (45 cm) apart, to create a more substantial

clump. *Heliopsis* cultivars flower from midsummer through to autumn (which is good value), and are fully hardy. Plenty of sunshine and an open situation is needed. Any fertile soil suits them, outside of a semi-bog situation.

Before specifying side-by-side companions for *Heliopsis* cultivars we should note that they are mid-border or back-of-border plants, because of their

BELOW This unusual
double form of heliopsis
is called 'Goldgrünherz',
which translates as 'gold-
green-heart'

BELOW Most heliopsis
cultivars are single, such
as *H. helianthoides*
'Hohlspiegel', photographed
here in mid-summer.

height. For the flowers to be seen to advantage they will benefit from some kind of background planting, preferably mid- to dark green in colour. They will also benefit from having plants in front to conceal the expanse of leafy stem between the flowers and the ground. These companions could range in height, but those immediately in front would need to be at least eighteen inches (45 cm) high.

The plants we might pencil in to provide suitable backgrounds will vary depending on the situation in the garden. There could be a yew or box hedge behind the border or, if space is no problem, a row of loosely growing evergreens, preferably those with a slight gloss to the leaf—for example, *Choisya ternata*, *Escallonia* 'Iveyi', *Itea ilicifolia*, *Osmanthus* × *burkwoodii*, *Viburnum tinus*, or (supposing you like them) various evergreen berberis, such as *B. darwinii*, *B. julianae*, or *B. verruculosa*.

To establish the colours of companion plants we must first admit that the yellow of *Heliopsis* is not a shy primrose, but a colour so brilliant as to be described by Graham Stuart Thomas as "blatant"—although he was biased against yellow daisies. To find companions for a range of *Heliopsis* cultivars, we could place them into one of three groups that were described in Chapter 14: first, the "creams-yellows-oranges-maroons-and-browns"; second, the

"exciting shades of bright pink, red, bright yellow, and bright orange" group; or, third, we could devise a grouping or scheme of our own. For the sake of example, let's explore the second option.

BRILLIANT IDEAS

Intensely coloured companions to accompany our first *Heliopsis* cultivar might therefore include bright clover-red *Phlox paniculata* 'Othello' , along with the dusky-red *Echinacea purpurea*. In front of these could go the acid-yellow fluff of *Solidago* 'Ledsham', with the orange-scarlet spikes of *Kniphofia triangularis*, dark red *Penstemon* 'Andenken an Friedrich Hahn' (commonly known as 'Garnet'), and the late-flowering *Geranium* 'Patricia' (magenta with a black eye). Dark glasses might be needed.

Our second *Heliopsis* could be grouped with the bright but subtle orange *Dahlia* 'David Howard', *Crocosmia* 'Lucifer', and the orange-brown *Helenium* 'Moerheim Beauty'. Smaller plants to accompany these could include yellow *Coreopsis* × *verticillata*, *Heuchera* 'Red Spangles' as well as the dusky pink *Origanum* 'Rosenkuppel'.

The next *Heliopsis* could associate, daringly again, with the magenta *Geranium psilostemon*, yellow *Senecio doria*, and orange *Hemerocallis* 'Burning Daylight', and in front of these could go scarlet *Penstemon* 'Schoenholzeri', yellow-and-black *Rudbeckia fulgida* var. *sullivantii* 'Goldsturm', pinky-red *Hemerocallis* 'Little Business', and the orange-scarlet Jerusalem cross, *Lychnis chalcedonica*.

Our fourth *Heliopsis* could associate with a *Eupatorium* cultivar, bright pink *Phlox paniculata* 'Eva Cullum', and dark red *Persicaria amplexicaulis* 'Atrosanguinea'. Additional tall perennials to partner with *Heliopsis* cultivars might include many other crocosmias, dahlias, and kniphofias; other *Phlox paniculata* cultivars, *Monarda* 'Cambridge Scarlet', fennel, and other *Hemerocallis* cultivars such as 'Stafford' (rich red with a yellow throat).

Annuals and summer bedding are often more brilliant and free-flowering than perennials, and would, therefore, add much to an eye-watering border such as this. Among likely candidates are *Alonsoa warsewiczii* (a tender subshrub with scarlet flowers), *Brachyscome iberidifolia* (bright purple), cleomes, sweet Williams, eschscholzias, heliotrope, impatiens, *Nicotiana* 'Domino Red', pelargoniums, petunias, French marigolds, and zinnias. Small foliage shrubs could prolong the season, including *Berberis thunbergii* 'Aurea', *Spiraea japonica* 'Golden Princess', or *Fuchsia* 'Margaret'—even yellow privet is not to be despised.

Let me hasten to add that if you prefer to be more cautious in your colour schemes then you could quite easily cool things down by adding blue, silver, and white to the border. In this case you would need plants such as violet-blue *Aconitum* 'Spark's Variety'; agapanthus, such as *A. campanulatus* 'Oxford Blue'; off-white *Aruncus dioicus*; sky-blue delphiniums; *Geranium* 'Rozanne'; silvery-blue *Eryngium* × *oliverianum*; *Lavandula stoechas* subsp. *pedunculata*; *Lychnis coronaria* 'Alba' (white-coloured flowers combined with silver foliage); grey-blue perovskia; low-growing blue *Phlox divaricata* subsp. *laphamii* 'Chattahoochee'; *Salvia officinalis* cultivars; and lacy-white *Selinum wallichianum*.

One thing is certainly clear—that by spreading the *Heliopsis* plants around the borders, as you would any other brightly coloured perennial, you

get through a lot of plants and use up a lot of garden by the time you've displayed a large collection.

LORDS-AND-LADIES

The second plant collection to be blended in among other plants is *Arum*. These are not to everyone's taste—in fact some gardeners think they're slightly sinister. Certainly there could hardly be a greater contrast with *Heliopsis*—the one bright, brash, and cheerful, and the other so reticent and mysterious. The strange "flowers" of arums require close

inspection to be appreciated, and even their greatest admirer would admit that they don't amount to much as contributors to the overall garden picture. From any distance at all, you would hardly notice them, except in the autumn, for their fruits. However, the yellow spathes of *A. italicum* and the palest lime-green spathes of *A. idaeum* will obviously show up more than the royal purple of *A. purpureospathum* and *A. palaestinum*, or the blotchy purple-brown of *A. dioscordis*. But the main problem is that when every other plant is present and standing to attention, arums have gone completely AWOL: during the summer months they are nowhere to be seen, being out of sight and dormant. So these are plants for the garden owner, rather than for the garden visitor—bearing in mind that summer is peak garden-visiting time.

Arums belong to group of genera called the aroids—members of the Araceae family—along with *Arisaema*, *Arisarum*, *Dracunculus*, *Calla*, *Zantedeschia*, and about a hundred other frost-tender genera—many of which can be grown as house or greenhouse plants. The hardy species are all low-growing, rarely more than eighteen inches (45 cm) high, and their only brilliance is the spike of fruits, which in some species are bright orange, and appear typically from late summer after the leaves have withered away. As monocots, they are sometimes included in books on bulbs, although their roots are better described as tuberous, or as a rhizome. *Arum maculatum*, the so-called cuckoo pint, or lords-and-ladies, is an extremely common British native along hedgerows and in woodland settings, but it is not very noticeable until the poisonous orange berries appear in late summer. The most common arum in cultivation is *Arum italicum* 'Marmoratum', which also has spikes of orange berries, and whose leaves are subtly and attractively variegated. Other interesting variegated cultivars of *Arum italicum*, though less commonly seen, include 'Chameleon', 'Bill Baker', and 'White Winter'.

The unusual construction of arum flowers has generated specialized terminology. Their flowers are very small and densely packed together in a vertical spike called a spadix, and this has a coloured bract

wrapped around it, called a spathe. The spathe is typically green, greenish-yellow, greenish-brown, or purplish-green—colours which are subtle, but liable to appeal to people (like me) who also like euphorbias, bupleurums, and umbellifers. The leaves of arums are more or less arrow-shaped—long and pointed—although the botanical description is not "sagittate" but "hastate", from the Latin *hastatus*, a spear. The genus *Arum* is distinguished from *Arisaema* by its undivided leaves (among other things): arisaema leaves are usually cut into three or more sections. The spathes of arisaemas also tend to be more hooded than those of arums, and are also more exotically coloured, though still fairly restrained.

Woodland soil is what suits arums best, and the fully hardy species are happy in light shade or sun. (The less hardy ones, mostly from the Mediterranean area, need a sunnier position.) They look best in a reasonably informal border with other woodland plants, not in a cultivated or contrived

OPPOSITE TOP The
hardy maidenhair fern,
Adiantum venustum, makes
the ideal partner for arums,
seen here in the author's
garden, with the fallen
leaves of *Photinia
davidiana* adding a little
colour to the scene.

OPPOSITE BOTTOM
Lamiums, such as the well-
known *L. galeobdolon* subsp.
montanum 'Florentinum',
make suitable associates
for arums, closing over the
gap when the arums are
dormant.

setting. A front-row position is needed, where they can be inspected at close quarters, but perhaps not the most prominent front-of-border spot in your garden—bearing in mind that the arums will not show up well from a distance.

It's not critical what goes immediately behind an arum, although plain greenery would provide some useful contrast. For this reason it would be a mistake to put a yellow foliage shrub behind the shapely yellow spathes of *Arum creticum*, and there would be no sense in putting *Arum italicum* 'Marmoratum' in front of variegated foliage. Dark glossy foliage will set off the orange fruits to maximum advantage: they look excellent with *Sarcococca hookeriana* var. *humilis*, for instance.

MINDERS, KEEPERS

To avoid bare front-row patches in summer, it's best to establish a partner or host plant that will cover the ground when the arums are dormant. I grow my own *A. italicum* 'Marmoratum' up through *Adiantum venustum*, which works well, but there are many other possible hosts. Small-leaved, trailing, non-variegated ivies could be used; other possibilities include the delicate, many-fingered leaves of sweet woodruff, *Galium odoratum* (formerly *Asperula odorata*); any of the lamiums; *Mitella breweri*, which has trailing stems and tiny yellowish-green flowers; *Vancouveria hexandra*, with dainty foliage and white flowers; any non-variegated *Vinca minor* cultivar; or small-leaved bergenias such as *B. purpurascens*. *Synthyris missurica* var. *stellata* (often seen as *S. stellata*), which has jagged-edged leaves and mauve flowers in late spring, would be fine

provided that the soil is not too dry. Epimediums and tiarellas might work, but their roots form rather dense mats that the arums might not appreciate. *Cornus canadensis* would be ideal in moist, lime-free soil, and among other such plants, *Galax urceolata* would be suitable, with its rounded glossy leaves, and also *Ourisia macrophylla*, the New Zealand mountain foxglove, with its evergreen foliage and white flowers in June.

Companion plants for a semi-shady position could include medium- or low-growing ferns, such the lacy and delicate, deciduous *Cystopteris fragilis*, or the glossy evergreen hart's tongue ferns, *Asplenium scolopendrium* Undulatum Group. Small hostas would work well in terms of maintaining interest— this would be a sequential rather than a synchronized association, since the hostas would be at their best when the arums were dormant, and would just be starting to wither away when the arum foliage returned. Spring bulbs could also be used—snowdrops, winter aconites, *Cyclamen coum*, and dwarf *Narcissus*. Among perennials one could try Solomon's seal (*Polygonatum*), pulmonarias such as the silvery-leaved 'Majesté', trilliums, *Anemone nemorosa* cultivars, *Iris foetidissima* 'Variegata', *Omphalodes cappadocica* 'Cherry Ingram', and shade-tolerant euphorbias such as *Euphorbia robbiae* and *E. amygdaloides*.

Host plants to grow with arums from warmer climates in a sunny site could include alchemillas, shorter forms of *Euphorbia cyparissias*, and cranesbill geraniums such as *Geranium* × *cantabrigiense* 'Biokovo'. Other possibilities are violas and the double chamomile *Chamaemelum nobilis* 'Flore Pleno';

Companions for these warmth-loving arums would again include spring bulbs, but the range could be extended to include *Muscari* and species tulips. Among suitable biennials and perennials are honesty (*Lunaria*), aurinias (formerly *Alyssum*) such as *A. saxatilis* 'Citrina' and 'Flore Pleno', corydalis, doronicums, smaller euphorbias such as *E. epithymoides* (syn. *E. polychroma*) and *E. myrsinites*, *Helleborus argutifolius*, and the orange vetch-flowered *Lathyrus aureus*.

It's worth noting that anyone wanting to grow arisaemas could plant them in similar associations to these described for arums.

THE TREE OF LIFE

Our third collection of plants needing partners and associates is a combined collection of dwarf varieties of *Thuja* and *Platycladus*. The range of shapes and outlines of these small conifers is somewhat limited

dicentras such as 'Snowflakes' (white) and 'Spring Morning' (pink) could also be tried, although they themselves tend to become dormant before the summer is over. Strong colours should be avoided, as these would overpower the arums.

LEFT Arisaemas are slightly more exciting than arums, but they can be handled in the same way as arums in the border. *A. ciliatum* in June, in the author's garden.

compared, say, with *Juniperus*. There are no carpeters, and almost all the dwarf forms may be described as "rounded", "bun-shaped" or "globular". *Thuja occidentalis* 'Caespitosa' is a particularly flat bun-shaped conifer, while *T. occidentalis* 'Ericoides' is similar in shape, but a larger and looser plant, with bronze-green juvenile foliage. Most types of soil suit *Thuja* and *Platycladus*, except badly drained or boggy conditions, and unlike *Juniperus* and *Cedrus* they will tolerate a degree of shade.

Any dwarf variety of *Thuja* or *Platycladus* with the description of "conical" will probably have a leading shoot, and although it may be slow-growing, it will eventually outgrow its "dwarf" description.

T. occidentalis 'Filiformis', for example, starts as a dwarf, rounded bush with strange thread-like foliage, but eventually becomes conical in shape and "medium" in height. *Platycladus orientalis* 'Hillieri' starts as an irregular ball of green mossy foliage, but increases by four inches (10 cm) a year, and slowly but surely after twenty-five years reaches ten feet (3 m) in all directions. However it isn't difficult to keep it small, as one can simply clip off the numerous spindly shoots it produces. *Thuja plicata* 'Rogersii' is an attractive dark green conifer, tipped with golden bronze, which also starts quite small, but only reaches about three and a half feet (1 m). Normally it's completely rounded in shape, but occasionally it throws out a leading shoot, and this needs to be cut off if the rounded shape is to be retained. *Thuja* and *Platycladus* both take clipping as long as it's not too drastic, and if they look like shorn lambs at first, they'll "come back" after a while.

From the garden-maker's point of view, these *Thuja* and *Platycladus* cultivars draw attention to themselves, in typical conifer fashion, in spite of being dwarf. In fact *Platycladus orientalis* 'Aurea Nana' could be regarded as the classic small conifer—distinctive in shape, neat in outline, compact in habit, and deserving to display its form to advantage. Halfway between rounded and conical, it is best described as egg-shaped. "Mini-specimens" is the best label for almost all of these cultivars, which look their best not with each other, but with unrelated lower-growing plants that don't compete with them for attention. In any case, all conifers are stand-offish, and don't like being touched on a long-term basis. Permanent contact with other plants causes

BELOW *Platycladus
orientalis* 'Aurea Nana'
(formerly *Thuja*), a virtually
egg-shaped dwarf conifer,
dominant at a small scale
and surrounded with low-
growing plants, that offer no
competition to the conifer.

unsightly dieback, and even if the offending neighbour is removed, the shape of the conifer may be permanently damaged.

Some dwarf conifers are regular enough in their habit in form to be planted in straight rows at regular spacings in a formal garden setting, as if they were dwarf box—although it's not that easy to discover just how fast-growing the various forms are, and which therefore will stay compact. I've had *Chamaecyparis lawsoniana* 'Gimbornii" for about twenty years, and now it's a complete, regular sphere approximately three feet (90 cm) across. *Thuja occidentalis* 'Danica' would probably behave in much the same way but, on the other hand, *T. occidentalis*

'Trompenburg' (from the Dutch arboretum of that name) makes an irregular mound of congested foliage, with sprays of scale-like foliage varying attractively in colour through the year. The less formal cultivars can be used in a mixed border where they can provide something of interest in the winter.

PROBLEM CHILDREN

Coloured conifers are more difficult to associate with other plants than green ones, and they don't mix very well with each other either. The impact of blue conifers can be softened by the inclusion of silver and grey foliage plants, although as it happens, there aren't many strongly blue varieties among

Thuja or *Platycladus*. *Platycladus orientalis* 'Blue Cone' is actually dark green, with purplish tints in winter, while *P. orientalis* 'Minima Glauca' is sea-green in colour. The bluest of these conifers is *Platycladus orientalis* 'Juniperoides', one of the soft-touch, juvenile-foliage forms, blue-green in summer and darker blue in winter.

Yellow conifers are more dominating and need to be used in moderation. To have bold shape and strong colour can be to carry attention-seeking too far. The small cultivars we are discussing here are not too strident, but tall yellow conifers are best kept off the Wants List. If you inherit one, you could try blending it in with lime-green or olive green foliage—admittedly not very common colours, but *Olearia nummulariifolia* is quite an interesting medium-sized, yellowy-green foliage plant I have in my own garden. *Cassinia leptophylla* subsp. *fulvida*, so-called golden heather, is another possibility, though rather leggy. The smaller *Phlomis chrysophylla* is a yellowy version of Jerusalem sage, while *P. leucophracta* 'Golden Janissary' is almost khaki-yellow, which sounds awful, but once seen does go straight on to the Wants List. The unusual foliage colours of *Bupleurum fruticosum* and *Ozothamnus ledifolius* could also be tried as buffers between golden conifers and the green of the rest of the garden. Alternatively variegated shrubs could be used, such as *Philadelphus coronarius* 'Variegatus', *Pittosporum tenuifolium* 'Irene Paterson', *Coronilla valentina* subsp. *glauca* 'Variegata', variegated box, or variegated hollies. Whatever you do, don't juxtapose yellow conifers with purple berberis, purple cotinus, or *Cercis canadensis* 'Forest Pansy'.

SEVEN DWARFS

Our first member of the collection looking for a partner or two could be one of the very dwarf cultivars—those of rock-garden size—such as *Thuja occidentalis* 'Hetz Midget' (mid-green in summer, with bronze tints in winter). This could have the knobbly-prostrate, one inch (2.5 cm) high *Sedum spathulifolium* 'Purpureum' in front, along with a *Sempervivum* such as 'Marmalade', 'Nouveau Pastel' or 'Dark Cloud', and silvery *Artemisia schmidtiana* 'Nana'. Larger companions could be added, such as the elegant dwarf *Penstemon pinifolius*, which has orange-red flowers in the late summer or early autumn (and dislikes wet), and the woolly-silvery mini-shrub *Helichrysum splendidum*, which has old-gold flowers for most of the summer (and is hardier than it looks).

We tend to associate conifers with the habitats in which they are found in the wild, and this can help us decide how we use them in the garden. In contrast to perennials, which come from prairies and clearings in deciduous woodland, coniferous forests are found in more rugged and mountainous country, less likely to be places of human habitation. This is why a conifer, even a dwarf one, can look out of place planted casually in a formal flower garden, or other places dominated by plants which are the result of horticultural selection and breeding. One traditional solution is to plant conifers with heathers, and although heathers are out of fashion at the moment, it actually works well. Heather moors and coniferous forests seem a reasonable match, even in miniature, and together they also create a very labour-saving garden. Dead boring, some would say, who like

more happening in the course of the year. But you don't have to make your whole garden into a conifer-and-heather display, even if you do have a dwarf conifer collection to house.

Our second dwarf conifer, therefore, could be planted in the late summer heather garden, among *Calluna vulgaris* cultivars such as 'Allegro'—dark green foliage and deep red flowers—or 'Anthony Davis', with light, grey-green foliage and white flowers. A plant with longer seasonal interest is 'Orange Queen', which would provide yellow foliage in spring, turning to orange in summer and deeper orange in winter, with suitably restrained pale lavender flowers. The problem with many heather gardens is that too many different cultivars are included, making the whole thing restless and unnatural. For a natural effect it is best if you can see only about three different cultivars in one glance.

Other carpeting plants could be added to this scheme—for example gaultherias (wintergreens) such as *G. miqueliana*, with pinkish-white flowers in spring, and pink or white berries in the autumn. Vacciniums could also be included, such as the amazingly hardy *V. macrocarpon*, the American cranberry, which makes good ground cover about four inches (10 cm) high; it has the interest of edible fruits, but needs soil that is not too dry. The low and creeping *Cotoneaster congestus*, with pinkish-white flowers and red fruits, might also fit in here. To provide height behind this carpet one could add tall heaths, such as the excellent *Erica × veitchii* 'Exeter', whose irregular shape will contrast well with the neat outline of the *Thuja* or *Platycladus*; alternatively *E. arborea* var. *alpina* would get even taller. A dwarf pine might also be appropriate, such as *Pinus mugo* 'Gnom', along with the dwarf rowan *Sorbus reducta*,

and *Salix lanata*, a good grey-leaved willow growing only three feet (90 cm) tall.

The next two or three members of the conifer collection could be planted in the lime-tolerant winter garden amongst *Erica carnea* cultivars, the classic being 'Springwood White' which was found in the wild in the Italian Alps, and has good apple-green foliage. 'Pink Spangles' is a fairly subtle bi-colour: cream and pink, fading to rose-pink. If we are tempted by coloured-foliage heathers, it's worth noting that some, like 'Foxhollow', don't flower, or at least only rarely: this does usefully avoid the clash of mauvey-pink heather flowers with yellow foliage.

We could achieve a little variation of height with the inclusion of one or two *Erica × darleyensis* cultivars, which are usually between twenty-four and thirty inches (60 and 75 cm) tall—more than double the height of *E. carnea*. 'George Rendall' has dark green foliage, with new shoots that are cream and pink in spring, and rose-pink flowers; 'Silber-schmelze' has silvery-white, scented flowers from well before Christmas. Taller heaths could provide a

background, such as *E. erigena* 'W. T. Rackliff', which has good green foliage and white flowers, or 'Irish Dusk', with slightly darker foliage and deep salmon-pink flowers. The foliage of *Ozothamnus ledifolius* would blend in well here, and to enhance the winter effect one could add a background of evergreen foliage with mahonias and *Sarcococca confusa*. To this one could add the coloured stems of *Cornus alba* 'Sibirica' (red) or *C. sericea* 'Flavi-ramea' (green), along with *Salix alba* subsp. *vitellina* 'Britzensis', which needs pollarding to give the best reddish stems.

HAPPY COMPANIONS

Any of the gold-foliage *Thuja* or *Platycladus* culti-vars, usually growing about two feet (60 cm) high, could be planted in a carpet of *Sedum kamtschati-cum* 'Variegatum', along with the St John's wort *Hypericum olympicum* f. *uniflorum* (also known as 'Grandiflorum'), which covers itself in bright yellow flowers, and a selected *Helianthemum* with orange flowers. Taller-growing companions could include the khaki-gold *Hebe ochracea*, the best of the whipcord hebes and ideal with dwarf conifers, and, for late spring flowers, *Daphne cneorum* 'Eximia' (possibly the best daphne), with deep pink flowers, and *Erysimum cheiri* 'Harpur Crewe', a perennial, scented, double yellow wallflower.

The bluest conifer in the collection, *Platycladus orientalis* 'Juniperoides', needs some protection, as its juvenile foliage can be damaged by frost and snow. It could be planted in an all-year-round grouping, surrounded by *Euphorbia myrsinites* (for late spring), silver-leaved helianthemums such as 'Wisley Primrose' (for early summer), *Sedum cauticola* 'Lidakense' which has bluish foliage up to four inches (10 cm) high and sugar-red flowers (in late summer), and the carpeting *Veronica prostrata* 'Blue Sheen', flowering from midsummer onwards. Taller plants to group behind these could include the elegant and early *Euphorbia rigida*, small blue hostas such as 'Halcyon', an eryngium such as *E.* × *tripartitum* (metallic and prickly), the dense masses of feathery grey *Artemisia pontica* and silver-white santolina, and the delicate stems of *Calamintha nepeta*, with its profusion of tiny flowers on branching stems.

A further member of the *Thuja*/*Platycladus* collection could be placed in a shady border to provide firmness and "body" among a froth of ferns and their associates. Suitable varieties would include *Thuja occidentalis* 'Woodwardii', *T. orientalis* 'Danica', or *T. plicata* 'Rogersii'. The conifer itself could be placed among fairly low-growing ground cover such as *Lamium galeobdolon* 'Silberteppich' or *Vinca minor* cultivars, and could associate with evergreen ferns such as *Dryopteris erythrosora*, or ferns that

disappear in the winter, such as *Gymnocarpium dryopteris*, the oak fern, and dwarf 'Plumosum' forms of *Athyrium filix-femina*, the lady fern. It would also be useful among dwarf hostas and trilliums, which also vanish in the winter.

Thuja/*Platycladus* varieties that are less formal in shape can be included in a mixed border. *T. occidentalis* 'Trompenburg' has already been mentioned, but also in this category are *Platycladus orientalis* 'Rosedalis', whose juvenile foliage is yellowish-green in spring, light green in summer, and brownish-purple in winter, and *Thuja plicata* 'Stoneham Gold', whose foliage is dark green where the sun doesn't reach it, yellow and bronze in the sunlight. These might hardly be noticed during the summer, when there are brighter plants around to take our attention, but they would come into their own in the winter, and would help to fill the border in early spring when it still looks quite bare. However, spring flowers could be added, such as aurinias, aubrieta, bright yellow *Euphorbia epithymoides*, early geraniums such as purple *Geranium libani*, *G. malviflorum* (which becomes dormant by late summer) or *G. sylvaticum* 'Mayflower', along with heuchera foliage, blue forget-me-nots, and scarlet tulips. These could be backed by the taller *Euphorbia characias* and perennial-friendly shrubs such as the dark spikes of *Hedera helix* 'Erecta' and yellow-and-apricot *Spiraea japonica* 'Goldflame'.

In case you hadn't noticed, it's worth pointing out that except for the first of these groups, which included a *Pinus* cultivar, none of these plant associations included the suggestion that one dwarf conifer could be planted next to another.

18
Some favourite genera

SOME GROUPS OF PLANTS are quite well known and popular, and this makes it relatively easy to build up a collection of them. Others, however, require some seeking out, the quest often being one of the pleasures of plantsmanship. Again, some plants are very easy to use in the garden, while others need careful placing, and it may therefore be helpful to note the characteristics of various plant genera, and how a collection of each can be successfully associated with other plants in the garden. Some of the genera below are included simply as examples of their type—a summer-flowering shrub, for example, or a tree with ornamental bark—and the advice given could apply to any similar genus.

ACER PALMATUM
Soil and space permitting, it's hard to imagine any drawback to collecting the many cultivars of this species. It seems to me that one could plant an almost endless array without anyone ever tiring of their shape, habit, or foliage. You can even grow them in pots.

ALNUS
Alders are not the height of horticultural excitement—in my opinion, they look at their best just before they come fully into leaf, when they take on a reddish tint. At Stone Lane Gardens in Devon, where there is a collection of alders along with a wide range of birches (*Betula*), the owners have livened things up a bit by mixing in a collection of bizarre and interesting sculptures among the trees. But if you aren't "into" sculpture, then you could perhaps divide the alders into informal groups of between five and seven trees (with no shrub layer), broken up by something quite different, such as *Ligustrum* or *Phillyrea*, using this block or bank of shrubs as a divider, rather than letting them spread beneath the trees, to allow the graceful forms of the alders to show up well.

ARTEMISIA
Most of the artemisias fall within a restricted colour range—grey-green to silver—and most have finely divided leaves. Although there is a wide range of heights, in most cases the overall shape of the plant is loose, rounded, and informal. Planting two artemisias next to each other doesn't seem to me to be a good idea—bread and bread, as they say. Better to have one artemisia and then a contrasting plant of some kind. Obviously nepeta would not be appropriate, being too similar to an artemisia, and the same would apply to a lavender, helichrysum, or santolina. What is needed is dark green foliage or, of course, flowers of any colour.

For flower colour, one could have *Artemisia alba* 'Canescens', for example, next to *Geranium* 'Johnson's Blue'. For foliage contrast, one could try *A. caucasica* beside khaki-coloured *Hebe ochracea*, or zinc-grey-green *Artemisia lactiflora* Guizhou Group against the evergreen leaves of *Prunus laurocerasus* 'Otto Luyken'. Alternatively, one could opt for textural contrast, and put *A.* 'Powis Castle' next to the smooth, dark leaves of *Acanthus mollis*. To create a contrast of form, one could place fluffy lad's love, *A. abrotanum*, behind bergenias, or lacy-leaved *A. stelleriana* 'Boughton Silver' next to the arching blue grass *Helictotrichon sempervirens*.

BELOW *Hemerocallis* 'Stafford', a well tried and trusted cultivar, seen here in a colourful mixed border. For an all-hemerocallis border see the illustration of one of the borders at Apple Court on page 49.

ASTER

Most asters flower between the first week in September and the middle of October, while a handful, such as *Aster × frikartii* and its cultivars, start several weeks earlier. When not in flower, asters don't offer much, since their foliage is rather dull. One or two asters have extremely dark leaves—for example, *A. lateriflorus* 'Horizontalis', but this is hardly exciting.

Planting all your asters together, therefore, puts you in a classic all-or-nothing situation—a dazzling display for a few weeks or so, with tedium stretching before and after—and to avoid this, it's better to dot your asters around the garden.

An example of an aster with two associating plants might be *Aster laevis* 'Calliope' placed alongside *Lobelia* 'Russian Princess' and *Anemone* ×

BELOW The National
Collection of asters at its
peak in the Old Court
Nursery, Colwall,
Worcestershire.

hybrida 'Whirlwind', and next to this a midsummer-flowering grouping, or else long-flowering plants such as penstemons.

On a larger scale, it would be easy to put a few asters together to form a pleasing group without creating too large a blank area in the border when they are not in flower. For example, an interesting group of asters of varied height could include the following: *A.* 'Little Carlow', *A.* 'Coombe Fishacre', two *Aster novae-angliae* cultivars, and an *Aster amellus* cultivar, but all these next to a grouping of earlier-flowering perennials.

ASTILBE

Apart from their colours, astilbes vary only slightly in size, and hardly at all in texture. About three astilbes together would be the maximum, I think,

before monotony would set in. Other plants with contrasting texture need to be inserted among them, such as rodgersias, ligularias, or hostas, their large leaves forming a contrast with the fuzzy-fluffy texture of the astilbes.

BERGENIA

The idea of grouping bergenias together is clearly absurd, as they all look exceedingly similar. Fortunately bergenias are sufficiently different in leaf form from most other perennials to make it easy to place them at the front of virtually any border. Bergenias can be planted in quite long bands, easily up to five feet (1.5 m) long, although eighteen to twenty-four inches (45 to 60 cm) wide would be quite enough. The sharpest contrast would be provided by more busily textured plants, such as *Nepeta*, cranesbill geraniums, or *Alchemilla mollis*.

BETULA

It is quite easy to imagine endless drifts of birch trees of different kinds, all looking quite pleasing, especially if nothing taller than about two feet (60 cm) was planted below them, so that their shape and elegant lines showed to advantage. However, you could occasionally break the succession of white stems with dark foliage, such as a band of the shrub-sized yew *Taxus baccata* 'Dovastoniana', a drift of choisya, or rhododendrons no bigger than six feet (1.8 m).

But birches are also useful blenders to insert among other trees, especially conifers, to provide variety and lightness. If time is on your side you can buy them very small and very cheap, and just wait for them to grow.

EUPHORBIA

Euphorbias come in a variety of shapes, sizes, and flowering times, but don't offer a wide range of colours. Apart from *Euphorbia griffithii*, which is orange, they are all yellowy-green. However, this colour is surprisingly easy-going, and fits into any imaginable colour scheme. One or two euphorbias are very strong-charactered, such as *E. characias* and *E. rigida*; *E. mellifera* is a superb foliage plant, but most are more average herbaceous plants, rounded in form. A group of three *Euphorbia characias* cultivars together might not be a good idea, as each would deserve to be a feature plant on its own. A group of three different euphorbias can work well together, however, provided that they flower simultaneously—such as *E. characias*, *E. epithymoides* (syn. *E. polychroma*), and *E. × martini*. However, one should bear in mind that the flowering times of euphorbias vary a lot—*E. cornigera*, for example, comes into bloom several weeks later than *E. characias*, and *E. sikkimensis* a few months later, and these would therefore be better planted with different companions.

GERANIUM

As fluffy greenery with delightful flowers, one could have about three geraniums together before you would begin to long for something with a little more bite. You might get away with assembling more of them if you set them within geometrical compartments edged with dwarf box, with the geraniums as filling in between. But otherwise, in the usual border situation, after several geraniums you need something firmer and more definite to give you a foliage colour break, such as santolina or *Hebe rakaiensis*, or else a specimen plant that is taller and bolder than the geranium, such as a large hosta, or else the broad foliage of an acanthus, the vertical spikes of an iris, or a specimen grass.

HELLEBORUS

Helleborus argutifolius and *H. foetidus* are excellent foliage plants, but other hellebores are quite boring out of season, since *H. × hybridus* cultivars don't have much at all to offer once they have flowered. You could perhaps have a group of about five *H. × hybridus* cultivars, possibly more in a woodland setting, but beyond that you would need a few ferns, hostas, or some other break from the dark green, or some other compatible plant with a lighter texture or a different foliage colour.

LEFT A candidate for any daylily-lover's Wants List—*Hemerocallis* 'Miss Jessie', a modern-looking and elegant "spider" daylily in pink and lemon yellow, raised as long ago as 1956 by Julia Hardy.

OPPOSITE LEFT *Hosta kikutii*, from Yakushima, and other islands south of Japan. It was named fairly recently after a Japanese botanist by the name of Dr Kikuchi.

OPPOSITE RIGHT *Hosta* 'Dorset Blue', with purple heucheras.

plenty of other plants that will—plants with contrasting texture, such as astilbes or thalictrums; plants with large leaves, such as hostas, Japanese anemones, or *Kirengeshoma palmata*; or plants with tall flower spikes, such as lythrums, persicarias, or *Lysimachia ephemerum*.

HOSTA

Hostas are best thought of as specimen plants. One wonderful hosta is a major statement. Two major statements is an embarrassment, like two presidential candidates on one platform. As for carpets of hostas, these make those of us with small gardens feel quite ill—and think of the awful mess they will be in autumn. He who has two plants of *Hosta sieboldiana*, let him give one away, and make room for something else. So, one hosta at a time is best, unless perhaps one is a giant and another is a miniature. Except for the tiny ones, they look best with smaller plants immediately next to them, along with perennials such as geraniums, astilbes, tiarellas, *Phlox divaricata*, or a shade-tolerant grass or sedge.

IRIS

Irises mean spiky leaves. Although they may not be fierce like phormiums, they are still vertical and pointed in shape. The various species need a wide range of differing habitats—some liking it warm and dry, others needing a waterside situation, and so on—so a collection of irises has necessarily to be scattered around to find the appropriate situations. Occasionally one sees a large sunny bed devoted to tall bearded irises, which looks good in bloom (obviously) but is boring for the rest of the year. And

HEMEROCALLIS

Daylilies might be described as exotically flowering grasses. The flowers bowl you over, but when they are finished you are left with the rather lax, strappy foliage, which is fine as long as you don't have too much of it. When they are young and recently purchased, three or more daylilies could easily form a group, but when they mature they form big clumps and you really only need one plant before you might want some variety. Obviously it's no good expecting grasses, liriopes, or kniphofias to give the necessary foliage contrast, but there are

if (like me) you are less than totally efficient, imagine the chaos if the labelling wasn't a hundred per cent accurate. At least if you spread your bearded irises around the garden you are less likely to lose track of which is which.

The vertical emphasis provided by iris foliage makes it ideal for creating contrast among other plants. The one proviso here is that the bearded irises like to have their rhizomes exposed to the sun, and if you put these irises next to a geranium, even a low-growing one, you have to be careful that the geranium does not creep into and shade out the iris rhizomes. But if you have annual forget-me-nots with irises, for example, sunlight will reach the base once the forget-me-nots have flowered and been pulled up.

Generally, bearded irises look best in a front-row position, among low-growing plants that don't compete for attention or light. Typical companions might be *Alchemilla conjuncta*, aubrieta, dwarf campanulas, cerastium, dianthus, *Hebe pinguifolia* 'Pagei', heucheras, golden marjoram, London pride (*Saxifraga × urbium*), sedums, or *Tanacetum haradjani*, although not all of these will necessarily be in flower at the same time as the iris.

KNIPHOFIA

When in flower, red-hot pokers draw attention to themselves more flamboyantly than almost any other perennial. It's true you could have a collection all growing together, but this would be like having a pack of cards consisting entirely of aces. It would seem a pity not to spread them around a bit, using them to create emphasis at certain key points in the garden—on either side of some steps, perhaps.

Like irises, kniphofias are useful for creating a vertical line in a border that is otherwise dominated by plants with rounded shapes. For a bit of excitement you could have a tall kniphofia, such as *K. uvaria* 'Nobilis', with a vertical phormium, such as 'Sundowner', and the airy, oaty heads of *Stipa gigantea*, with *Kniphofia* 'Johnathan' next to the vertical heads of the tall grass *Calamagrostis × acutiflora* 'Karl Foerster', backed by the towering stems of *Eryngium pandanifolium*, and with a dwarf kniphofia, such as 'Bressingham Comet', at the base, along with *Carex buchananii* and *Libertia peregrinans*.

PAEONIA

Peonies are here today, gone tomorrow. It's worth waiting fifty weeks to see their flowers, reminiscent of

gorgeous ladies of a bygone era, but after a couple of weeks all you have is leaves. The foliage is quite good, but the stems tend not to stand up too well after the flowers have gone. As rule, I'm against "squeezing in"—giving a plant slightly less space than it deserves—but if ever there was a plant to be squeezed in between later perennials, it is a peony.

PENSTEMON

I could cope with quite a lot of penstemons before I got tired of them, and what is more, the colours all blend, which is quite an achievement considering that there is quite a wide range of colours available. Multicoloured drifts of these long-flowering perennials are very easy on the eye. However, at Kingston Maurward, in Dorset, they have their penstemon collection in beds divided with dwarf box and this works well, imposing some order on the layout.

PHILADELPHUS

A philadelphus is a big, rounded hummock of dreary green, which for a few weeks of the year has little white flowers which dot the greenery. The flowers are deliciously scented, but opinions differ: some find the perfume overpowering. Even so, three of these shrubs would be the most you could tolerate before boredom overwhelmed you, after which you would need something of the order of *Mahonia* × *media* 'Charity' to jolt you back into paying attention to the garden.

PHORMIUM

Phormiums are attention-seekers, and a whole border of them would be like the annual parade of some hostile tribe—only appreciated by those who enjoy aggression. Spread round the garden as punctuation marks to liven up a dreary group of philadelphus or shrubby loniceras, for example, they are very useful, but a border with too many phormiums would be too ferocious. While the variegated and reddish phormiums tend to be carefully named, if you wisely just want a green one, it seems you are at the mercy of chance as to what you'll get from the nursery.

PINUS

Pines can be planted in drifts all of one species, or alternatively as specimens, so that you can see the shape of the individual tree to advantage. When pines of many different kinds are planted too close together the result can be unsatisfactory, although for understandable reasons this commonly happens, even in the best arboreta. When those tiny saplings were planted decades ago it was hard to imagine what giants they were going to turn into. It would be a crime to plant anything underneath pines, unless of course it was a few thousand cyclamen.

RIGHT A variegated
phormium in a town garden
in Gloucestershire. A cultivar
of small to medium size, the
stiff, vertical spikes softened
by the shapes of the
surrounding greenery.

POTENTILLA

Shrubby potentillas make rounded humps, covered in flowers over a long period. I particularly like the silvery-leaved ones. They don't mix particularly well with each other, however, as this creates the effect of several humps set side by side, but if several of one kind are planted close enough together to make what appears to be one much larger plant, they look fine: this is the landscape architect's approach to planting. In winter they are not very attractive in my opinion, looking like dead brown bears, but some people like them.

ROSA

There are roses and there are roses, and it seems to me that roses of different types don't usually blend satisfactorily together.

Hybrid teas and floribundas say "horticulture" to me and need a different location from the big, informal shrub roses, with their more sprawling, less domesticated habit. As a general rule, a collection of hybrid teas, floribundas, or smaller shrub roses benefits from some kind of structure to the layout as a whole. A rose bush is a shapeless thing, and if you have a whole gang of them they need a bit of discipline if they are to look at all reasonable: setting them out in rows or in rectangular beds usually helps. Sissinghurst in Kent is as near perfect as you can get in this regard: the beds are geometrical in design, the content of the beds is informal, and there is plenty of companion planting. Loose island beds don't work so well for roses, because then you have shapeless objects in a shapeless setting with nothing holding it all together. However, unkempt giants such as *Rosa moyesii* enjoy a much wilder setting, where chaos can have free reign.

UMBELLIFERAE

Several umbellifers are collectably statuesque, such as angelica, *Ferula communis*, and *Molopospermum peloponnesiacum*. But umbellifers come in quite a range of sizes and some, such as hacquetia, are quite diminutive. Flower colour is mostly limited to white, but a few are yellowy-green and one or two of the white ones have cultivated pink forms. Several flower slightly ahead of the main summer display, but more awkward are the species that die down too early for convenience, leaving large gaps in the late border. Others "go off" (or, in other words, don't look all that good once flowering has finished). A group of three different species could look attractive planted together, but more than that might leave an area that looks a bit tacky later in the season. In general they are best dotted about the garden, and as with peonies, one feels tempted to squeeze the smaller ones in here and there.

Index

PHOTOGRAPH LOCATIONS (page numbers)
(11) private garden Gloucestershire; (14 above) Mrs Valerie Merritt's former garden, Gloucestershire; (16) private garden Gloucestershire; (23) Mr & Mrs Peter Heaton's garden, Wotton-under-Edge, Gloucestershire; (29) Cotswold Garden Plants, Badsey, Worcestershire; (30 above) Old Rectory, Duntisbourne Rous, Gloucestershire; (30 below) The Garden House, South Devon; (40 bottom) Mrs Margaret Baber's garden, Lydney, Gloucestershire; (42) Mr Dennis Moorcraft's former garden, Gloucestershire; (45) Mrs Isabel Grindley's garden, Gloucestershire; (46) Old Rectory, Duntisbourne Rous; (47 above) private garden in Surrey; (48) private garden in Gloucestershire; (52 below) private garden designed by the author; (53) Mrs Valerie Merritt's garden; (104) Sizergh Castle, Cumbria; (144) St Egwins Cottage, Norton, Worcestershire; (171 bottom) Beth Chatto Gardens, Essex; (173) Iden Croft Herbs, Kent; (177) Lady Farm, Somerset; (178 bottom) Beth Chatto Gardens; Mrs Valerie Merritt's garden; (182) Mrs Mary Byrne's garden near Cork, Ireland; (211) Rosewood Daylilies, Canterbury, Kent; (215 left) Mr Dennis Moorcraft's garden; (217) Mr David Richards's garden, Gloucestershire.

FOOTNOTES
(page 10) 1 Gerard Manley Hopkins, *Pied Beauty*.
(page 95) 2 *Hillier's Manual of Trees and Shrubs*, by Harold G. Hillier, first published 1972.
(page 110) 3 Don Witton manages to hold a first-rate euphorbia collection by growing them on his local authority allotment (intended for vegetables) near his house, in Yorkshire.
(page 136) 4 At the Country Garden garden centre, Windlesham, Surrey. Collection holder M. Harwood.
(page 185) 5 First published 1908; reprint of the 1936 edition re-issued by the Antique Collectors' Club, Woodbridge, England in 1983.